Topiary

DESIGN AND TECHNIQUE

Topiary

DESIGN AND TECHNIQUE

Christopher Crowder and Michaeljon Ashworth

THE CROWOOD PRESS

First published in 2006 by
The Crowood Press Ltd
Ramsbury, Marlborough
Wiltshire SN8 2HR

www.crowood.com

British Library Cataloguing-in-Publication Data

A catalogue record for this book is available from the British Library.

ISBN 1 86126 816 5
EAN 978 1 86126 816 7

Line illustrations by Claire Upsdale

Typeset by Servis Filmsetting Ltd, Manchester

Printed and bound by Replika Press, India

Contents

(i)

PEACOCK LEVENS GARDENS.

(iii)

(ii)

Kendal, In Levens Hall Gardens.

(iv)

157.
Levens Hall Gardens.

(v)

Introduction

A [topiary] garden . . . the place

Where good men disappointed in the quest

Of wealth and power and honours, long for rest;

Of having known the splendours of success,

Sigh for the obscurities of happiness.

William Wordsworth

My first recollection of topiary is at Levens Hall in Cumbria, where I was captivated by its mystique and whimsical Alice in Wonderland atmosphere. Many plants in my parents' garden subsequently suffered as I experimented with my own ideas of topiary. Now, having travelled the gardens of Britain and Europe and eventually come home to make a garden in my middle age, my impact on plant material is more informed and creative and topiary has become a hobby. The garden at Levens has become a close friend and a reassurance that no matter how small my own garden is there will always be somewhere that topiary can be luxuriated in and can be used to create a contemporary garden in spite of the historic setting. I see the specimen topiary figures as animate beings engaged in desultory or occasionally philosophical conversation with each other. Usually they gossip, and thanks to the state-of-the-art bedding which surrounds them and constant stream of visitors from around the world they speak in the current idiom and also in just about every language.

Its history intrigues me, for as a garden historian I look for recurring themes and images that have survived the test of time; in topiary I have found an icon which signifies 'garden' throughout all time. I am in Arcadia with the Greek shepherd watching his flock nibble shrubs into pleasing shapes, I am with his wife who dries her linen on those smoothed plant surfaces, and I am also with the priest who planted such a shrub in his sanctuary. I am also – and most importantly – in my own garden sanctuary snipping away at box plants asking them to tell me what shape they would like to become.

There are many topiary gardens but only one Levens Hall. I hope that this book guides everyone interested in topiary both practically and inspirationally.

Michaeljon Ashworth

We wish you well if you choose to enrol in that long, long line of topiary gardeners to which we both belong. We can guarantee both success and happiness as well as the surprises inherent in any creative art. Topiary makes an artist of the gardener in us and it is with gratitude to topiary itself that this book is dedicated, for without it clipping, snipping and pruning would be but necessary chores. Topiary by its very presence transforms gardens into something extra and other – but, above all, magic.

OPPOSITE PAGE
(i) *Old postcard of Levens Hall showing a peacock next to specimen topiary, and the determination of the postcard printer to show the topiary icon of the clipped bird.*
(ii) *Old postcard of Levens Hall showing the triumphal arch commemorating Queen Victoria's Diamond Jubilee in 1897. It is actually rare to be able to date a piece of historic topiary so easily.*
(iii) *Old postcard of Levens Hall.*
(iv) *Old postcard of Levens Hall.*
(v) *Old postcard of Levens Hall.*

CHAPTER 1

History

The history of topiary is as long as the history of gardening itself. The hand of man upon a single tree, shaping it to please and demonstrate his control over nature is an icon that symbolizes the very genesis of gardening. This green thread of aesthetic pruning leads right back in time to the wall paintings of ancient Egyptian tombs with their colourful representations of practical horticulture in cool, shady enclosed spaces away from the dusty heat of that other world outside the garden. Early images of trees shaped artistically differ from trees depicted in a stylized manner, which is proof of the antiquity of topiary. It may well be that workers skilled in the productive pruning of fruit trees according to the horticultural calendar were redirected to more creative work during slack periods.

In searching for the origins of topiary, and indeed of ornamental gardening, it is relevant to consider the ordered symmetry and striking form of evergreen Mediterranean cypresses and of palm trees in Egypt and Mesopotamia. These forms translate readily into domestic cultivation in the case of date palms and into an ornamental, heavenwards exclamation mark in the case of the striking cypress – decorative and productive plant forms close to human habitation. It is not a great leap to transfer the symmetry that occurs naturally in the pencil-thin cypress to other attractive evergreens. The sound of clipping in the garden echoes back to that first application, a sound that reverberates around a surviving topiary garden like Levens Hall for almost half of every year.

Likewise it could be speculated that hedges originated in areas lacking an abundance of wood for fence construction, where ditches used as barriers and filled with water for irrigation encouraged the natural growth of shrubby material in lines along their banks. Rather than remove the plants, people soon realized they were useful in maintaining the banks of the ditch by preventing erosion. Cleaning and tidying would prevent encroachment on both ditch and growing area. Again, it is a leap of imagination to transfer the practical application of a

Mediterranean cypresses in their natural and distinctive shape. The genesis of topiary is in the observation of symmetry and significant form in trees growing naturally.

Russell Page's informal topiary with low mounds of myrtle under standard orange trees. This Italian garden is a setting for spring bulbs, with tulips replicating the standard 'lollipop' shape of the orange trees.

clipped line of shrubby material to the ornamental garden space inside the courtyard of a dwelling place. For year-round decorative purposes evergreens would always be preferred, with a predisposition towards native plants or exotics that could be easily propagated in order to guarantee the quantity required.

ROMAN TIMES

It was in Roman times that documentary reference was first made to the *ars topiaria*, or art of topiary, as an elaborate, highly stylized and sometimes over-the-top status symbol for the sybaritic villa life associated with Pompeian decadence. The word 'topiary' itself derives from Latin and the writings of Pliny the Elder. Initially *topiarius* referred to the illusionistic wall paintings that added false perspective to the enclosed gardens of Roman villas. They can be seen magnificently today as survivors of the AD79 eruption of Vesuvius and record the then prevalent ideas regarding what constituted a pleasing landscape and garden features. Pliny refers to the representational aspects of topiary. Clipped box could display the name of the gardener or owner of the villa, or could represent animals, battles and heroic characters from history and mythology. Complex and labour-intensive, this plant art clearly appealed to the Roman sense of taste and was achieved by the Roman dependence on slavery.

Archive photograph from Levens Hall showing the scale of work involved in maintaining historic specimen topiary – and the need for a head for heights.

History repeats itself in this contemporary nursery specimen of a jumping horseman often mentioned in old documents. This ready-made piece needs nothing but maintenance and shows the contemporary enthusiasm for topiary.

Pliny the Elder described 'hunt scenes, fleets of ships and all sorts of images' in cypress in his *Natural History*, which is a long way from the tall, slender outline of the plant growing naturally. It is not a great leap forward to Disneyland. What is clear is that topiary was common in the upper echelons of society and from surviving accounts high status 'villa society' could not get enough of it. This cachet was enhanced by Pliny the Elder attributing the 'discovery' of topiary to one Gnaius Mattius, a friend of the Emperor Augustus, who was most unlikely to have ever held a pair of clippers in an era of mass slavery. Rather like a general claiming a triumph as reward for a foreign conquest it is more feasible that Mattius simply took the credit for the diffusion of a gardening style imported from older civilizations beyond the Roman Empire. His approval in imperial circles would have counted for much and inspired the political allegiance of the emperor's followers to be demonstrated in their gardens. The same thing was to occur later in the history of topiary when the arrival in England of William of Orange in 1685 stimulated the creation of specimen topiary gardens as Dutch gardens – a lesson from classical Rome in how to clip one's way into favour.

The shaping of plants (principally box) as low hedges to edge beds and form complex patterns as well as to articulate garden space is impressive and is a recurring theme in garden history, seen in knot gardens, parterres and mazes. Specimen topiary shapes and decorative figurative work may seem frivolous rather than functional but do illustrate two important things about topiary: the first is that despite the durability and tolerance of the plant material used there is always the possibility to change it. The names of people spelt out in box could always be altered if ownership or stewardship were transferred. As for the green sculpture of figurative topiary, that could quite easily be left to grow out of one manifestation and turned into another. The decadence of the Roman Empire is the ultimate cliché of the flight from boredom. This is a great advantage of topiary – its adaptability.

Aerial view of the King's Privy Garden at Hampton Court showing the symmetry of formal parterres containing sculpture and topiary.

The other point is that in topiary there can never be any illusion that the material used is anything other than plant material. It may be sculpture but it is made from living green plants, evident to all who care to inspect it close up. Such living material, like the hairs on the head or the beard on the chin, requires constant attention.

Ultimately nothing shows the value placed on topiary more than the fact that it was formulated, written down and taught and passed on. A tradition was established, specialized tools were developed, or at least adapted from other cutting treatments such as sheep shearing, and the scope for imaginative gardening was greatly increased. The Romans probably invented the garden makeover.

Pliny the Younger, nephew of Pliny the Elder, described his own villa garden in Tuscany. Its contents included topiary animals cut in box, a lawn surrounded by an evergreen hedge, a circular area with box figures at its centre, a carefully clipped shrubbery 'prevented by the shears from running too high', a knot garden of dwarf plane trees, separate rooms, a meadow (wild garden), an orchard punctuated by topiary obelisks and 'numberless' box figures cut formally juxtaposed against an imitation of the 'negligent beauties of rural nature'. This menu is totally resonant with gardening as it is known and practised today. Clear design, spatial division and the contrast of formal and naturalistic create a linked series of different experiences.

Topiary is a prime example of a feature that, having passed the almost imperceptible tests which govern success and favour in gardening, has

A Dutch garden showing the classic, standard orange tree 'lollipop' in a Versailles planter.

Medieval knot garden showing the pattern laid out on the ground and topiary letters, numbers and figures in the surrounding palisade. The human figures dwarfed by the garden and the simulation of an aerial view represent man's domination of nature, which is ultimately greater than himself.

Old postcard showing the view over the topiary garden at Levens from the upper storey of the hall.

survived to become a constant factor in the repeatedly rekindled love affair between the garden designers of the western world and the infinite garden heritage of the ancient world, as exemplified particularly in Italy. We can only speculate about the appearance of gardens such as Pliny the Younger's but the survival of the art of topiary is our link to its very existence. Topiary has survived not only the dramatic events and upheavals of history but also the vagaries of fashion and predilections for innovation, bolstered by its enduring popularity with gardeners everywhere. The current widespread revival of interest in the practice of topiary is a testimony to its continuing attraction.

THE MIDDLE AGES

In the delightful garden scenes of mediaeval manuscripts topiary reappears in the *hortus conclusus*, a garden very often imbued with religious symbolism and dedicated to the Virgin Mary. The tiered, cake stand and fountain forms suggest both control of and respect for nature, isolated and therefore extremely noticeable in the manuscript miniatures. These illustrations are rare prior to 1400. If the question is asked as to how gardening survived the so-called Dark Ages then the answer is that civilization and its offspring gardening were confined within the cloisters of monasteries in western Europe and continued to contribute to the fabled city of Byzantium.

Once western Europe emerged from the Dark Ages, mazes, labyrinths and bowers were created in secular and chivalrous settings. The arbour or 'herber', a shady walk between two parallel hedges joined overhead to form a roof and often leading to a suitably situated bower, required serious pruning as fast-growing lime was often used. The Fountain Garden at Levens is a recent example, and removed as it may be from the romantic notions of bowers and trysting venues in bowers, hedges could often grow so densely that it was possible to walk on top and thus get a view. At Levens again, the double beech hedge, which resembles nothing less than three centuries of condensed tree growth, provides its own scaffolding for supporting planks to permit clipping work. However, in our insecure world of health and safety concerns, the public, romantically or otherwise inclined, are unlikely ever to be allowed to walk aloft it.

The Italian Renaissance, with its spirit of cultural rebirth and reappraisal of antiquity, filled the history of gardens with formal evergreen creations alive to this day with the sound of clipping. One only has to look in the backgrounds of Renaissance paintings to see tiered and shaped evergreen trees extending into what is obviously the natural world

A mediaeval lady appreciating cake-stand topiary, taken from a manuscript margin.

Archive photograph of the beech hedge at Levens Hall. This hedge defines the longitudinal axis of the garden, contains an inner walkway and divides the garden into separate areas.

Historic garden showing repeated motifs of tiered topiary and circular beds with single tulips – a delightful lesson in garden design. The covered arbour walk is shady and the circular beds are a shape repeated in the tiered topiary centrepieces.

outside any man-made architectural space. This suggests the artist, living and working in a studio in the town, had an inbuilt, almost archetypal, image of a tree as being topiarized. Looking at works such as Leonardo da Vinci's *Annunciation* (in the Uffizi in Florence) or at the spectacular frescoes in the Palazzo Medici-Riccardi (also in Florence), you get the impression that Renaissance Italy was filled with a landscape of clipped trees outside any dedicated garden space. Gazing into the hazy, dreamlike backgrounds of paintings shows us how artists thought trees were expected to look. It is just like asking a small child to draw a tree from a repertoire that contains a lollipop and a Christmas tree.

Italian Renaissance gardens containing topiary are very often restored and recreated after the passing of so much time. Villa Gamberaia is a perfect example of this. Recreation in contemporary terms is a recurring theme in gardens. In a sense the annual clipping of historic specimen topiary is a recreation dependent on growth, damage and tool management. Box, cypress, laurel, myrtle, ilex and yew are tough evergreens, chosen for the extremes of the Italian climate. Castello Ruspoli and Villa Della Petraia demonstrate an Italian preference for topiary as parterre. This was not always the case and historical evidence supports an early revival of Classical Roman figurative and specimen work.

At Castello Ruspoli box has been planted in gravel to make a pattern on a terrace; such planted patterns have to be viewed from above.

Italian Renaissance fresco showing topiary trees in the background replicating the design of the fountain in the foreground garden. While no one can say that trees in the landscape were topiarized, this illustrates that the image of a tree in an artist's head was of a topiary specimen.

Hypnerotomachia Poliphili, printed in 1499, is always heralded as the first printed book to show intimate garden spaces containing both classical sculpture and topiary. The black and white woodcuts leave no doubt as to which is which, for however much topiary contorts it never disguises its organic nature. The author, a monk called Francesco Colonna (pseudonym Poliphilius), wrote of and illustrated imaginary gardens that contained a vast range of box peacocks, hyssop spheres, pleached screens, shaped junipers in pots and parterres of trimmed herbs: santolina, lavender, marjoram, rue, artemisia and thyme. His book also shows the human form in topiary, and all told is a spectacular dream catalogue of visionary gardens.

That it influenced contemporary garden design can be in no doubt. The Rucellai Garden in Florence describes what amounts to the theme park of the book: 'spheres, porticoes, temples, vases, urns, apes, donkeys, oxen, a bear, giants, men and women' were all formed of evergreens (various but not specified) bound to withy frames, a fifteenth-century reference to technique. Presumably the frames fixed the ultimate dimensions as well as defining the shape.

The 1930s model garden created for an exhibition in Florence draws on such literary accounts. Whoever creates a topiary squirrel, battleship or elephant today is paying into the deposit account of garden history as a homage to what has been done before. The inspirational aspect of historical topiary cannot be better emphasized than in the above description. The garden is nor an indivisible entity but a collection of complementary features. To create one piece of topiary art is to become a 'green sculptor' as well as a bona fide subscriber to ancient tradition! However, tradition must not eclipse the spirit of delight in which topiary was always received. It is fun in an ingenious and artful manner.

A classic Italian Renaissance parterre in box at Castello Ruspoli showing the detail and depth of pattern created by light and shade.

One of the fantastic designs clipped in box derived from Hypnerotomachia Poliphili.

This unique model of a Renaissance garden made in the 1930s shows imagery – elephants surmounting the hedges – that recurs in literature from Pliny to the eighteenth century and clearly draws on written sources in its design.

THE TUDORS AND STUARTS

Appropriately it is in the time of Greensleeves and Shakespeare that topiary first entered the vernacular of the English garden. It had started its life in England much earlier in two dimensions as the knot garden, derived from the simplest of labyrinths and edged parterres. This low boundary for herbs and flowers in clipped box could become an end product in itself. In entwined and three-dimensional ribbons of box it became a striking and complex feature, much appreciated today as a challenge. There is an illusion that the ribbons of box do continue when they pass under each other, but they don't. The patterns that knot gardens display can also be seen on strapwork plaster ceilings, dress fabrics and architecture, as they were very much a cultural feature of the age. These patterns have been successfully and beautifully reproduced in contemporary gardens, while the simple parterre of box edging has found new life in the potager.

Topiary seems to capture and embrace the idea of an Elizabethan garden, whether as a knot garden or as a clipped specimen. Whether box is or is not a native plant in England, it is relatively rare and localized. According to John Parkinson in *Paradisus in Sole Paradisus Terrestris*, 1629, box was in fact considered a curiosity, and for knot gardens hyssop, germander, thyme and armeria were used which suggest a very flattened form, while ligustrum was preferred for vertical topiary.

The recreated knot garden at Little Moreton Hall, Cheshire is a simple design reflecting the architecture of the Tudor house perfectly. It is surrounded by beds edged with box and containing standard gooseberries, which had been used ornamentally as far back as the reign of Edward I in 1275, imported from France.

The sixteenth century saw a great surge of gardening as life became more peaceful (provided one's religion was not out of favour). Henry VIII set the pace with his acquisition and development of Hampton Court. A German visitor, Platter, in 1599 described the Privy gardens, where he saw centaurs, servants with baskets, figures of men and women all wrought in topiary. There is even documentary evidence of bonus payments made to gardeners who were diligent in making knots and clipping them – incentives to specialization and a realization that standards of maintenance were important, as indeed they still are.

At this time there is a pleasant bias towards women in garden writing. When William Lawson wrote *A New Orchard and Garden* in 1618 it was written for country housewives. This indicates a probable division of labour, with the husband out

Contemporary knot garden created using different varieties of box.

Russell Page's green gardening creates an abstract pattern emphasized by Italian sunshine.

in the fields and the house and garden the responsibility of his wife. In what one would imagine to be a labour-intensive world a different picture emerges when the 'country housewife' is told, 'Your gardener can frame your lesser wood to the shape of men armed in the field, ready to give battle; of swift-running greyhounds, or of well scented and true running hounds to chase the deer or hunt the hare.' The 'well-scented' (that is, created out of aromatic herbs) hounds perhaps suggests this is a little tongue in cheek and in any case is directed at the woman with time to read. Barnaby Googe had written *Foure Bookes of Husbandry* in 1577, wherein he mentioned the popularity of rosemary, especially among women who trimmed it into 'the fashion of a cart, a peacock and such things as they fancy'. A point to remember in this context is how important hedges were to housewives for drying and bleaching laundry. Sadly, the importance of what we read from this time is inversely proportional to the little topiary that actually survives.

Testing the practicality of what is written is a mark of its veracity. For example, Parkinson comments on the invasive nature of box root growth and suggests using an iron blade to cut through them where they spread into a planting bed. This practice continues today with the use of a broad and sharp spade.

An 1874 Gardeners' Chronicle *engraving of the topiary walk at Levens Hall. There is a topiary look to the ladies in their Victorian dress, and the dog has clearly found what looks like a kennel.*

As topiary became more and more fashionable it is perhaps not surprising that dissenters appeared. Francis Bacon, in his essay *Of Gardens,* 1625, wanted nothing to do with knot gardens intended to be enjoyed from upper windows. 'They be but toys: you may see as good sights, many times in tarts.' For anyone interested in creating a contemporary knot garden the point about their being designed to be seen from above is extremely useful. Most of us do not have reception rooms on an upper floor, and when viewing a knot garden from the ground at eye level a complex pattern is superfluous. Bacon's was a lone voice for many years; besides knot gardens he disliked images cut out in juniper or other garden stuff: '...they be for children. Little low hedges...with some pretty pyramids I like well, and in some places fair columns.'

His reference to low hedges and pyramids is an exact description of the seventeenth-century garden recreated at Levens Hall in Cumbria. The simplicity and clarity of this design is what John Evelyn referred to as 'hortulan architecture'. Simple geometric shapes with vertical emphases lining a terrace walk or delineating a parterre essentially form the framework of formal and architectural gardening over three centuries. The filling in of these outlines has changed with fashion, as different styles of parterres became bedding out, and labour-intensive bedding out was replaced by turf or gravel until contemporary planting was introduced. History creates a back catalogue of solutions irrespective of fashion and compromises, since mergings and mixings are all viable solutions when no particular period is favoured. Taste is personal and often judicious while fashion is copycat and rapidly becomes weakened through diffusion.

At this point it is worth remembering that the maze is a garden feature that ought to be considered as an elevated extension of the patterned knot gardens. Deriving its intricacy and element of quest

A seventeenth-century parterre showing the flowers used subservient to the overall design in box.

Recreated seventeenth-century garden with flowers, using circles and edged with box punctuated by topiary cones.

Contemporary view from above showing the topiary garden at Levens Hall rising above carpets of blocked, monochrome bedding. Topiary needs a setting, and bedding allows for changes to be rung twice a year.

from distant antiquity a maze (invariably of dense yew) is nothing less than three-dimensional interactive topiary. Neither architectural nor functional as we might describe a box edging, or indeed any hedge, it belongs to the pleasure garden as a fixed game feature. However, as it has a history and a symbolism beyond that of topiary, and with its mythological and religious origins it is better to exclude it from this work. By its very size and scale the maze belongs in the grand and historic gardens, and in its contemporary manifestation as a feature cut out of a field of maize has become almost an agricultural pun.

The received image of a historic topiary garden was created in its most recognizable form by the end of the seventeenth century. In 1652 the garden at Packwood House in Warwickshire was planted with the yews that as an ensemble have become known as the Sermon on the Mount. Specimen topiary and its groupings have always invited quests for symbolism or been given pet names. There is never a right answer. Many topiary pieces with their all-round symmetry and sculptural form can be considered to resemble gigantic chess pieces. The Packwood yews are a case in point, where tradition and affection, as well as the fact that there is a row of twelve to suggest the apostles, conspire to promote a legend.

John Evelyn in *Sylva* (1664) endorsed the use of yews. This book, intended as a practical guide to forestry, suggests transplanting them at three years, which means beginning with relatively small plants. 'Form them into standards, knobs, walks hedges etc, in all which works they succeed marvellous well and are worth our patience for their perennial verdure and durableness. I do again name them for hedges, preferably for beauty.'

This could be John Evelyn's endorsement of the garden he never saw at Levens Hall, which has become probably the most famous and certainly the most complete seventeenth-century topiary garden to survive and thrive.

That Evelyn opted for yew is interesting, because by the 1680s bad winters had seen off cypress from the Mediterranean countries as a reliable topiary subject in England. Historic specimen topiary is invariably made with yew, as it is quite simply the best plant for the job. In selecting yew, strong growth and verticality are guaranteed in what – compared to box – is a tree rather than a shrub.

Levens Hall's ornate specimen topiary has its origins in the gardens of Holland, Belgium and northern France. What might be considered as frivolous or just fun topiary was the challenging work in human and animal form. Looking back at Italian gardens as recorded in illustrations there is yet another strand of topiary that is parallel to the exotic contortions suggestive of metalwork and glass formed into terminal features. Obelisks, finials, spires, balls and pyramids suggest both geometric formality and in most cases a strong verticality. Above all they emphasize three dimensions and the capability of being seen 'in the round'.

This specimen topiary was certainly a feature of the grandest gardens, as the palace of Versailles testifies. The inclusion of it on such a large scale here

Old postcard of Levens Hall.

An 1874 Gardeners' Chronicle *engraving of the topiary garden at Levens Hall, showing the variety of forms in the specimen topiary. The figures moving around inside the topiary garden show the importance of accessibility, and the surrounding planting is clearly herbaceous.*

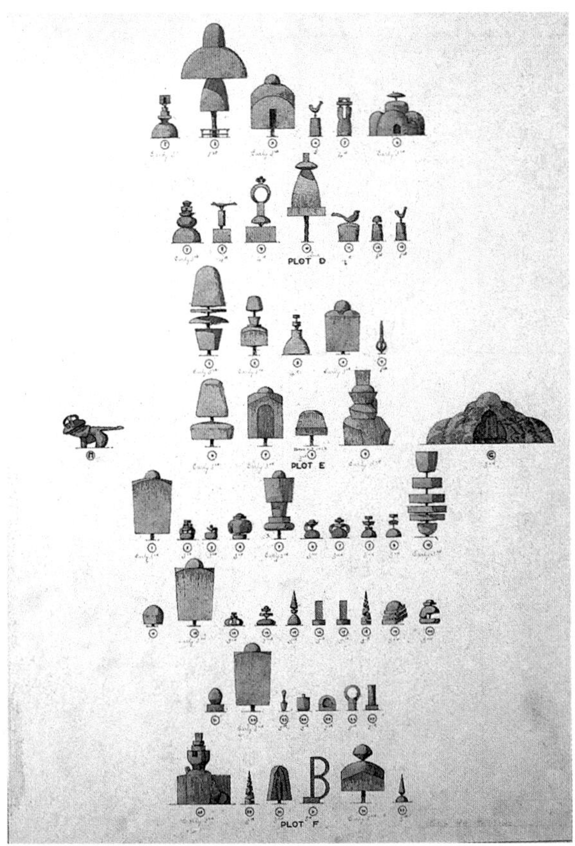

A 1920s catalogue of the topiary designs at Levens Hall. Catalogues of designs survive from Versailles in the seventeenth century and what is clear is that variety of design was important from the start, as plants had to be trained from an early stage.

implies that nurserymen cultivated plants specifically for topiary and in a range of embryo shapes that could be transplanted, grown on and maintained as strictly as was necessary in their final location. They were also a long-term commitment requiring annual clipping and a clear, strategic understanding of the desired form.

THE GEORGIANS

While Versailles is today seen as a vast palace and vaster garden offering tourists a historical (and exhausting) seventeenth-century experience, contemporary England naturally did not look upon the Sun King's domain in quite the same way. Versailles represented absolute monarchy and Roman Catholicism, so the British looked instead towards the protestant Netherlands. Charles II had stayed there in exile, and ultimately William of Orange and his wife, Mary, daughter of James II, transferred Dutch court life and culture to England when they succeeded James II in 1689. Topiary, a typical feature of the Dutch garden, could send out acceptable messages of political and religious adherence. The roads leading to Levens therefore begin both at Versailles and in Holland.

The gardener at Levens Hall from the 1690s was William Beaumont (or Guillaume de Beaumont, who had worked under Le Nôtre in France). After the collapse of the Stuart line, topiary began to

The surviving Dutch garden of William of Orange at Het Loo in the Netherlands.

symbolize adherence to the new Dutch regime even though there was a historical native tradition. Topiary gardening became Dutch gardening. The wonder of Levens is the quantity and variety of original specimen topiary that was preserved, for soon the winds of fashion were dictating the appearance of topiary everywhere, only to change when inevitably the Dutch style reached saturation point. The garden at Levens became a Noah's Ark for preserving specimen topiary. Its distance from London and changes in fashion as well as considerations of expense and expedience left it alone. A garden such as Levens Hall has survived for many reasons, but above all it is due to the successful concentration of specimen and architectural topiary there that the garden has remained complete and been maintained to the highest of standards.

At the peak of its popularity the Brompton Road nursery of London and Wise, founded in 1681, provided the plants and advocated topiary. Their production overtook the initial importation from Holland. William Hazlitt described their speciality as 'that preposterous plan of deforming Nature by making her statuesque, and reducing her irregular and luxuriant lines to a dead and prosaic level through the medium of the shears. Gods, animals, and other objects were no longer carved out of stone; but the trees, shrubs and hedges were made to do double service as a body of verdure and a sculpture gallery.' On the face of it Hazlitt seems repelled by the artificiality of topiary, but interestingly it is also possible to read a grudging admiration into his remarks; certainly he was writing at a time when too much topiary, bad topiary, the use of unsuccessful plants and too much frivolity was starting to turn the tide of taste.

Topiary gardens in Britain are usually compared with Levens, the great survivor. For more than

Archive photograph of the topiary garden at Levens Hall.

Archive photograph of Levens Hall showing the topiary walk with its parade of different shapes.

three centuries the long-cherished topiary shapes have successfully withstood all the changes in gardening fashion and are fixed features in surroundings that have responded to planting changes in gardening styles. The idea of fixed points as permanent features around which to garden is an inspirational concept for contemporary gardens.

When you look at illustrations of newly planted old topiary gardens, the topiary specimens are invariably skimpy and insignificant; as they grow the primary aim has to be not so much to adhere strictly to a sharp outline than to respect the proportions and layers of the original intention as far as the fuller growth permits. This factor of scale is totally relative and readily shaped specimens sold today are probably not far from the optimum size required in the small garden. The giants of history have their setting in grand gardens. The seventeenth-century topiary at Powis Castle in Wales has with time lost all sense of identifiable shape and has become smoothly clipped amorphous forms that soften the formality of the baroque terraced garden under the castle.

The contemporary gardener investing in a garden today is not attempting to contribute to historical posterity but is searching either for a relatively low-maintenance striking feature or an instant effect around which temporary planting may be introduced and changed. The rise and success of makeover gardening has created a market prepared to invest in larger specimen plants for instant effect. Suppliers of topiary specimens respond to this demand and for the enthusiast the challenge of starting with a tree and directing it into a shaped specimen is perhaps too demanding when it is possible to procure a plant already directed towards a clearly identifiable form.

A cone becoming a tiered specimen as its growing tip has been allowed to grow up and separate into two areas of vegetation.

Large topiary specimens in a nursery. While this is instant gardening, it is also costly.

The fashion for Dutch gardens was relatively short-lived. Evaluating the style suggests that it was suited to smallish, cottage gardens and that on a grander scale it was French gardening by another name. The restored Westbury Court in Gloucestershire charmingly evokes all that was Dutch about the Dutch Garden. Colonial Williamsburg in the USA emotively evokes William and Mary old England in a superb setting.

Topiary famously exposed itself to ridicule in the early eighteenth century. A reaction against topiary gardening arose in tandem with the rise of the natural landscape movement. It was also an indication that topiary became considered old fashioned and in bad taste. In elitist circles the very fact that examples of topiary could be found as single specimens in cottage gardens as well as in royal gardens was frighteningly egalitarian. This ambiguity of status was ridiculed by the style counsellors as was the shift away from continental influences. Yet the ridicule heaped on topiary is essentially inspirational because the offending articles are a catalogue of ideas. In the early eighteenth century, essayists were regarded as the authority on all that was modish. Joseph Addison launched his attack in *The Spectator* in 1712. 'Our British Gardeners... instead of honouring Nature, love to deviate from it as much as possible. Our trees rise in Cones, Globes and Pyramids. We see the Marks of the Scissors upon every Plant and Bush. For my own part, I would rather

A cottage garden overflowing with topiary including both cake stand and heraldic designs (a boar's head and a peacock).

A topiarized oak in a hedgerow. When topiarized, boundary trees cease to present potential problems of outgrowing their location in the garden.

The cottage garden at Chatsworth recreates the topiary furnishings described in seventeenth-century sources and is amusing, imaginative and a solid demonstration of the success of directing growth over frameworks.

look upon a Tree in all its Luxuriancy and Diffusion of Boughs and Branches, than when it is thus cut and Trimmed into a Mathematical Figure.' Any admirer of a topiary garden could only find this critique both inspirational and worthy of an enthusiastic response. Any gardening follower of fashion and taste in 1712 might have felt uneasy.

What is not derided here (perhaps because beneath contempt) is figurative topiary. It was in the following year, however, in Alexander Pope's essay in *The Guardian*, where he describes how '...we seem to make it our Study to recede from Nature, not only in the various Tonsure of Greens into the most regular and formal Shapes, but even in monstrous Attempts beyond the reach of the art itself: We run into Sculpture, and are yet better pleas'd to have our Trees in the most awkward Figures of Men and Animals, than in the most regular of their own...A Citizen is no sooner proprietor of a couple of Yews, but he entertains Thoughts, of erecting them into Giants...I know an eminent [Mr] Cook, who beautified his Country Seat with a Coronation Dinner in Greens, where you see the Champion flourishing on horseback at one end of the Table and the Queen in perpetual youth at the other…'.

Pope famously and facetiously fictionalized a catalogue of specimens on sale at an eminent Town-Gardiner's, which include 'St. GEORGE in Box; his Arm scarce long enough, but will be in a condition to stick the Dragon by next *April.* A *green Dragon* of the same, with a tail of ground-ivy for the present. N.B. *These two not to be sold separately.* A Lavender Pig with Sage growing in his Belly and a NOAH's Ark in Holly, standing on the Mount; the ribs a little damaged for want of water.' Pope's assumption is that such features are not appropriate to 'polite' gardening. He was having fun at the expense of topiary and its followers, and at the same time showing up the paranoia of dictated taste.

The last laugh is on those who chose to deride this art form for what they are describing as being beyond the pale and what is being enjoyed in the eclectic world of contemporary gardening is the fun element in topiary, just as it was in Classical Rome. Fun and gardening did not really go together in the first half of the eighteenth century. Nature was to be taken seriously. While fun was out if it was planted, it was perfectly acceptable in the pleasure gardens established and open to paying customers for all forms of consumption, dalliance and performance. Topiary was on the carpet for not respecting Nature, and a linear patterning of the ground with the embroideries of the grand parterres was swept away in great haste by the mid eighteenth century.

The landscape movement and its leader Lancelot 'Capability' Brown was in the ascendant. What it did was shift the focus of gardening away from the domestic surroundings of a country house into the larger landscape. This expansion actually ensured the survival of some old topiary gardens because their comparatively small scale made them unlikely candidates for the improvements of Capability Brown and his followers. By 1772 Sir William Chambers warned that if 'the mania were not checked, in a few years there would not be found three trees in a line from Land's End to the Tweed'.

The great advantage of yew and box is that if it goes unclipped and is neglected then it quite

Old postcard of the topiary walk at Levens Hall.

simply grows out into a tough native plant, particularly box. The longevity of yew and its regenerative powers permit it to survive a century or so of neglect.

Just as the pendulum swung against formal and topiary gardening it also returned. In 1803 Humphrey Repton challenged the whole philosophy of the landscape movement. 'Why this art has been called "landscape gardening" perhaps he who gave it the title may explain. I can see no reason, unless it be the efficacy which it has shown in destroying landscapes, in which indeed it seems infallible.'

THE VICTORIANS

The return to favour and revival of topiary is part of the story of English gardening in the nineteenth century. Nothing is missed more than what has been lost. In 1794 Uvedale Price in *An Essay on the Picturesque* condemned both Brown and Repton as well as admitting to having destroyed an old-fashioned garden himself: '...I doomed it and all its embellishments, with which I had formed such an early connection to sudden and total destruction..., I remember, that even this garden (so infinitely inferior to those of Italy) had an air of decoration, and of gaiety arising from that decoration.'

The British are a nation of amateur gardeners instilled with images of what constitutes a garden and what does not. Price is anticipating these continuers of the tradition by referring to a garden, alas lost, as having been a place of decoration and gaiety. In grand gardens the formality of Italian gardens was reintroduced, with clipped evergreens adding to the architectural features of balustraded terraces, fountains and statuary.

At the same time an increasing number of owners of smaller gardens started seeking links with traditional gardening and provided a fertile ground for the quiet comeback of topiary. This revival was romantic and emblematic of the artistic and literary gardens described in Pre-Raphaelite paintings or Tennyson's poetry. It responded to the advocacy of William Morris and the Arts and Crafts Movement. The sound of the clipping of evergreens returned to the garden. Sedding, an architect favoured by Morris, had a love of gardens founded in the Italian Renaissance.

'Of the gardens of Italy, who shall dare to speak critically? Child of tradition: heir by unspoken descent, inheritor of the garden-craft of the whole civilised world. It stands on a pinnacle high above the others, peerless and alone: fit for the loveliest of lands...splendidly adorned, with straight terraces, marble statues, clipped ilex and box...so frankly artistic, yet so subtly blending itself into the natural surroundings.' This was written by an architect who included much topiary in his gardens. He recognized quality and the importance of distinctive garden features as well as appreciating nature as a background.

THE TWENTIETH CENTURY

The garden as it is recognized today entered the twentieth century on a raft of inspirations. Topiary was revived and seen to chime in with Oriental gardens, bonsai being the most extreme expression of topiary. The Japanese strand of topiary included Cloud Topiary and the rolling landscape 'green rocks' of *bonseki* much appreciated in the USA, where there were less dogmatic fashion shifts and openings for innovation.

Two firms furnished the public with 'off the peg' topiary specimens. Cheal & Sons in Sussex and William Cutbush & Son in Highgate, who surely had a name to trade on. Old photographs show their exhibition grounds crammed with birds, spirals, boats and tables shaped from yew and box. Cutbush travelled in Holland, purchasing surviving and ancient specimens from the Boskoop area, which was famous in the late seventeenth century for specimen topiary. They had survived around old farmhouses and formery nurseries and ended up sold as Cutbush's cut bushes.

The industrial age's cult of the idealized Romantic Olde England had returned topiary to favour as an iconic feature of gardens. Victorian 'Jacobethan' revival houses very often transported and restored old yew trees that had formerly been topiarized and were centuries older than the houses they were to grace. It was in 1904 with Curtis and Gibson's *The Book of Topiary* that the first history of topiary was published as a monograph. This was published in the gardening world that had seen the foundation

Old postcard of Levens Hall showing a bird and a tiered specimen framing a view of the gardener's cottage. Representation and abstraction are side by side (or back to back) here.

of *Country Life* magazine 1895, which even took topiary images of clipped birds as its editorial page logo. The National Trust had been founded as the vanguard of a conservation movement which in time embraced gardens. By 1925 and Nathaniel Lloyd's *Garden Craftsmanship in Yew and Box* the survival and revival of topiary was almost guaranteed. Nathaniel Lloyd reminded gardeners everywhere that the imagery of topiary was a perfect foil to repro gardens idealizing the past. Still, topiary had yet to survive the Second World War and its aftermath. Country houses and their gardens did survive the war and, what is more, opened their gates to the public at large. An enormous upsurge in gardening has subsequently entered the mindset of the nation. Towards the end of the twentieth century gardening had become the province of everyone. Topiary is a pleasurable way of adding distinction to a garden and its sculptural and structural emphasis is within the reach of all who can take up a pair of clippers. Topiary has happily returned to fashion, which means that publications and garden centres can supply its inspirational and practical needs at a time when pleasure in gardening is propagated by the media and television in particular. This brings the story into the twenty-first century and the topiary of today as an inspiration for amateur gardeners wishing to enter that long, long tradition of clippery.

History is continuity and remembrance. Visiting historic gardens is never like visiting museums, for what is growing there is alive now rather than bringing the past to life.

CHAPTER 2

Inspiration

New topiary was born out of the current love affair with gardening. Television makeovers and personalities from those programmes enthuse a population to garden for pleasure, or at least to make a garden and live in it. The cultivation of one's garden has become a cult and topiary plays its part.

It is helpful here to divide topiary into three different subdivisions: old topiary, new topiary and art topiary. These do not reflect any historical timescale but are simply categories into which your various options fall. Old topiary consists essentially of surviving historical models which contemporary designs may either copy or be based upon. New topiary broadens the use of the art form and places it in containers, brings it indoors or indeed respects the material itself and becomes a free-form sculpting of plant material. Art topiary is very often concerned with decoration and floral art rather than just the integration of shaped plant material into the garden itself. It can be tremendous fun in itself as well as being decorative and festive. Each of these categories owes a debt to the past, which connects its manifestations and creations to the green thread of clipped artwork rooted in antiquity. How the tradition continues and expresses itself depends on the contemporary world's relationship with plants and gardens.

Looked at another way, topiary divides naturally into two groups: architectural topiary and sculptural topiary. Making this simplistic but clear distinction offers no indication of the artistic content and quality of the results obtained. Topiary is an artistic outlet and therefore is in the hands of the artist, who may wish to respect the style of the existing house and its garden or expand its artistic potential into new areas.

Detail of topiary animals with cat, duck, elephant and Mickey Mouse.

Mickey Mouse, close-up.

ARCHITECTURAL TOPIARY

Architectural topiary is essentially the creation of 'walls', as in hedges, which may mark boundaries or screen anything from a wheelie-bin to a garage. The walls may join up to form a covered bower or structure or follow a line to become a hedge. When planting a hedge it is the horticultural skills that are most important to ensure the rapid growth of the chosen species. This will be referred to in more detail later.

There are hedges and hedges, and the massive blocks of yew buttressing each other in their 'upholstered' squashiness at Renishaw Hall have a life and a movement which at ground level suggests privacy and security and an aching desire to see what they are concealing. Hedges may demarcate boundaries but they are also green dividing walls to break up a garden into rooms and separate experiences. When the garden space being hedged or enclosed is small enough to be considered as only one room, then any irregularity or variation in the silhouette of the hedge can add more interest; for example, a projecting buttress hiding part of a flower bed or lawn gives the added value of surprise and anticipation.

Inspiration for small-scale contemporary gardens is so often derived from the close scrutiny of details and small areas of gardens visited; this in

A semicircular arcade both encloses space and opens windows on to views of Florence in this restored Renaissance garden at Villa Gamberaia.

Summer bedding in mats of colour under the specimen topiary at Levens Hall. The blocks of colour complement the topiary masses.

Crisply cut massed topiary shapes.

Amorphous topiary shapes showing precision clipping over curved surfaces. These could possibly be chess pieces but what they definitely are is a tribute to the art of the topiarist.

fact requires that the garden visited, while working as a whole experience, needs also to be subjected to highly charged maintenance and manicuring in its particulars. It is this standard of detailed maintenance which makes a garden open to the public worth visiting. Photographs taken for inspirational purposes are usually of details, and the part captured in the image is very often a stylistic summary of the whole. This reduces a large garden to a part which can then be comfortably transposed to a smaller, domestic setting.

The Serpentine beech hedge at Chatsworth is the perfect example of a hedge not having to be straight. Even if it follows a straight boundary the inner side can undulate. No more does the top surface of the hedge have to be flat – it can be scalloped into waves and grown up and out into sculptural details at will. The illusion of fully rounded topiary emerging from a hedge is a space-saving ploy and saves the effort of having to create a free-standing piece in the round. Undulating, amorphous hedges out of which slightly more distinct shapes semi-emerge are an inspired and extremely engaging way of working in topiary. 'Amorphous' means a non-geometric shape so the light, rather than striking planes, curves over rounded forms that create shading and depth in their undulations.

Tapered yew columns growing out of a hedge at Renishaw Hall frame a fountain and contrast strongly with the white abutilon. With age they have started to bulge and seem to swagger with personality.

Topiary walk with half shapes emerging from a hedge.

Topiary buttresses flank the entrance to a double herbaceous border. This view from Arley Hall, Cheshire, shows the forceful and striking imagery of matching pairs and symmetry used architecturally.

MAZES

The ultimate manifestation of the hedge as linear architectural topiary is certainly the maze. This ancient tradition with its mystic, mythological and religious associations is scarcely an inspiration to the vast majority of gardeners today, but is certainly worthy of admiration, and symbolically for the small gardener emphasizes how misdirectional paths can increase the sense of space in a garden. Translated into topiary hedging terms, a couple of staggered screens can break up a smallish garden into varying prospects.

Miniature hedges, usually in box, are the dividing boundaries of potagers, parterres and knot gardens. In the first two cases the small hedge divides and contains growing areas. It has to be stated that miniature box hedging used as edging is neither cheap not trouble-free, and is a major investment when done extensively. Santolina and lavender are certainly cheaper and can add a silver edge to sunny locations. Lavender is rather less formal and also produces scented flowers.

Box is traditionally associated with gravel walks, and gravel is now often seen in gardens replacing

The 50-year-old double serpentine beech hedge at Chatsworth is a symphony of movement as it flows with the undulations of a wave in a straight line across the garden.

front gardens as a less successful car parking surface than brick paviours, or indeed replacing grass lawns as a low-maintenance option. While gravel needs to be confined by a secure border in tile or wood its perimeter can be enhanced by box edging or an alternative plant species.

Gravel is a perfect foil for topiary. Indeed many recreated historical knot gardens use only gravel and grass to fill the interstices of the box parterre. The revival of topiary and the widespread use of gravel (or similar stone surfacing materials) in gardens today invite the patterned edgings and knotted ribbon work of the traditional parterre. Indeed the scope for inspiration is vast, with Celtic linear artwork providing in itself a wide repertoire of scrolls and interlocking patterns, ranging from simple spirals to complex designs. It is rather like tattooing a gravel garden with linear box, and speaking of tattoos reminds one of Pliny talking about names being 'grown' in topiary work. Whether linear and on the ground ('par-terre'), or three-dimensionally upright and sculptural, it is one way of signing a garden makeover.

Tall hedges are boundaries and screens, knot gardens and parterres planted in patterns on the ground are low hedges used internally within the garden. The hedge is one option for enclosing the garden space and defining or disguising its boundaries. Nevertheless, as it stands and grows as

Topiarized hedging in superb condition and almost architectural in detail. This resembles a post-modern pediment.

Topiary shapes emerging from a hedge.

quickly as possible it is very much functioning as a wall. Patterned gardens are therefore flooring and a filler of garden space, thereby defining the style and design of the garden. There is a long-term commitment with a parterre and an evocation of the past, which may or may not be appropriate to the house or the uses its owners may wish to make of their garden space.

Contemporary spin and inspiration to enthuse the topiary gardener can be found when the above-mentioned division of topiary into architecture and sculpture is merged and obscured. Such inspiration

Birds on drums flank the entrance to the central path of the topiary garden at Levens Hall.

Formality and symmetry in a topiary parterre of green and golden yew. The hemispheres of golden yew soften the stunning architectural form of this topiary container at Chatsworth.

has its roots in the historical development of abstraction in art and the liberation of garden design from a constant reinterpretation of its own historical precedents.

SCULPTURAL TOPIARY

Sculptural, specimen topiary with the shaping of plant material to greater or lesser degree is the most awe-inspiring and evocative form of topiary. 'I came, I saw and I marvelled' is a frequently felt response of visitors to historic gardens, who then return home to smaller gardens decorated with scattered bicycles and laundry carousels. Specimen topiary can be inspirational in two forms: in dramatic isolation, or grouped and fused into composite forms, invariably abstract and amorphous, which derive from oriental and American influences. In effect, the merging of abstract topiary

Summertime view over the garden at Levens Hall.

Tiered specimen with scrolled head-piece.

creates its own landscape form and its contours harmonize with its surroundings.

Isolated Features

An isolated vertical green feature plant or tree growing in the centre of a lawn or gravel or paved area can have great dramatic effect. What it has going for it is the solid, year-round interest of an evergreen. Anyone who thinks that looking the same all year round is rather boring needs to spend a year following the play of sunlight on evergreens wet and dry throughout the calendar. No plants are more responsive to atmospheric effects, changing skies and that occasional and magical dusting of snow. With yew in particular there is also the contrast in colour when it is clipped between the new shoots and the old growth. (Incidentally, a vertical specimen topiary only needs clipping once a year, which leaves plenty of time to enjoy its changes throughout the seasons.)

The strong silhouette of whatever shape – tightly geometric, freehand or figurative – has an imposing presence in the garden. Nowhere is a better place to hang lights at Christmas and in a front garden given over to car parking it can be the one strongly individual feature that reflects the individuality of the property owners.

Inspiration to create the monolithic verticality of a single specimen on a single stem can be derived from the traditional English, Dutch, French or Colonial American garden. Such a specimen is very much a variation on the tree as a symbol, with a symmetrical shape rather like the trees on an ordnance survey map or a child's imagined Christmas tree. It is very often claimed in guide books that many historic specimen topiary examples were intended to be representational, but in fact many such references are affectionate later appellations drawing on resemblances (for example the Twelve Apostles at Packwood). While there is a striking similarity, say, between standard chess pieces and topiary specimens it is perhaps better to accept that each age has its own characteristic images and forms which recur throughout the arts. Specimen topiary when paired adds the balance of symmetry to a house and garden. When grouped it can add depth and texture. Representational topiary is invariably unmistakable, however much the intended peacock may end looking more like a turkey! The topiary peacock has long been the symbol of the English cottage garden, adding a note of contrast between an aristocratic bird and a humble dwelling. As history has shown, however, the repertoire of representational topiary shapes is almost limitless and only restricted by the space available and the imagination of the gardener.

Eastern Influence

Other sources of inspiration that ultimately lead on to more contemporary examples of topiary can be found in the orient. It is ironic that the contemporary mindset and its 'New Age' affinities is closer to the expressions of Zen philosophy than to mediaeval and classical allusions. The advantages of

Snow on topiary adding the magic of Christmas card land to the topiary garden at Levens.

Light and shade emphasize the three-dimensional strength of topiary.

Contemporary view at Levens Hall showing sculptural juxtaposition of green forms.

Peacock in Lonicera.

Obelisk in a white Versailles tub against an old brick wall. Container topiary works well as year-round evergreen interest against the walls of a house. You can ensure even light distribution by rotating the container during the year.

Classic standard in a Versailles tub. This iconic tree shape is a work of art, and like all topiary demonstrates the importance of all-round access and attention.

Japanese (and Chinese) influence is that Zen gardens offer maximum inspiration from minimum content. Clusters of three amorphous, freehand clipped evergreens (or even deflowered rhododendrons carefully maintained as foliage evergreens rather than flowering shrubs) set in a sea of gravel or raked sand with accompanying rocks strike a note of mystery and abstract minimalism, which, coupled with the low maintenance for such an arrangement, has a very strong and gripping appeal. Without being initiated to a religious cult the visual impact is lucid and strong. Japanese topiary images rise vertically with the spectacular cloud pruned topiary of branching stems leading through 'clouds' of foliage to other terminal 'clouds', all in all taking up little precious ground space as the densely manicured 'clouds' float like bunched balloons above the ground. Freehand and amorphous though it might appear, this is highly disciplined work.

The Western interest and enthusiasm for the container-gardening style of bonsai – which is surely the ultimate in topiary art in the extent of its control over plant material – is a reminder that containers are an acceptable and desirable home for topiary large and small. There are many examples to be seen and purchased ready made of multiple-headed box, for example, or lonicera, which look both ways and fuse the traditions of East and West.

Rows of young specimen topiary in a nursery bed. Divided according to their initial shape, tiered individuals can be seen at about the age of six years.

Nursery specimens. The ready-made peacocks are an example of instant gardening, just waiting to be set in a smooth green lawn.

A teddy bears' picnic with invited squirrels. This shows the joy of topiary and the fun of wire-framed models en masse.

Topiary in containers is not new. The classic Georgian town house front door flanked by matching Versailles tubs containing standard bay trees is a familiar image and indeed is regarded as an icon of high taste. Standard plants are available in a vast range of species and tend to be bought ready grown. Apart from raising flowers closer to the viewer's eye they are extremely effective when grouping pots as they add a vertical accent. While strictly speaking being topiary within its broadest remit, flowering standards are beyond the scope of this work.

Container topiary evergreens are moveable and can be arranged in pleasing groupings and played with, perhaps used temporarily until a permanent and acceptable configuration is arrived at before planting them into the ground. Containers can also be 'buried' in gravel areas.

GETTING STARTED

Contemporary topiary interest is fed and nourished by nurseries and garden centres. Inspiration is one thing but guidance and confidence are far more important. The range of plants available and the accessibility of basic forms or embryo specimens in topiary makes starting up relatively easy.

You can buy chicken-wire frames and outlines for figurative topiary and train suitable plants over, round and through them. Arty, festive and very decorative animal shapes can be used as gifts and commemorations and once installed in a garden or on a patio usually lead on to further additions.

Decorative topiary, such as ivy spirals, table-top box balls, cones and standards and bonsai cloud topiary are very desirable for parties and weddings.

Inspiration can be drawn from history, from garden visiting, from Japanese gardens, from abstract shapes and patterns, from representations and from the whimsical eccentricities of the imagination. It has traditionally been seen as a way of exercising control over nature and engaging trees and shrubs in a dialogue with man conducted in terms of formality, representation and the rhythm of repetition and conformity. Outside these traditional confines abstraction and land art create more organically inspired work, responding to the shape of the plant and the lie of the land.

Whatever the inspiration it will always depend for its success on the good practice of sound gardening principles. Artistic expression has always been about truth to materials and in topiary gardening the soil, climate and attentions of the gardener must all interact to produce the desired results in the best possible way.

Massed topiary as a backdrop to yellow antirrhinums at Levens.

CHAPTER 3

Assessing the Site

Topiary can be used in many ways and is a gift to the inspiration-led or inspiration-seeking gardener. It may be formal or informal, traditional or contemporary, abstract or representational, permanent or temporary (for example, topiary decoration in marquees and churches for weddings), or in the case of container-planted examples, mobile. Mobile topiary, like bonsai, is often the instigation of a collection and the pleasure derived from arranging and staging compositions or groupings of pots. It also means that topiary may be carried as a gift and placed on a table indoors for temporary decoration.

The initial assumption here is that investment is being made in topiary specimens growing directly in the ground as permanent features of a garden design, although much of this chapter will also be relevant to container cultivation. Firstly it must be stated that topiary, like hedges, needs to be considered to be a long-term, even permanent, feature in a garden. Consequently you need to give due

Box spheres en masse in a nursery field. There is beauty in repetition and this range of specimens illustrates the current demand.

attention to initial planting, location and establishment of the plant so it can be an investment that will provide long-term pleasure and benefits in the garden. Skipping over these matters lightly can lead to failure and, given the expense of large, specimen plants, even financial loss not to mention the tragedy of a blank space occurring where a plant has died in a prominent position. Every garden is different but the need to dedicate thought, time and energy at the start of the project is the same for everyone, and resources spent now can only repay with great effect over the years to come.

CLIMATE

Climate needs to be taken into consideration from the start in both the choice of plant material to train and individual topiary design. You have little if any control over the general climate of your area, but as every gardener will know each garden expresses its individuality in possessing a microclimate. It is perfectly possible to look over the fence, or rather a manicured hedge, and see a plant succumb to frost, wind, drought or waterlogging while the same species survives on the home side of the boundary. This is a factor to be exploited and needs careful assessment, as these small localized variations may make all the difference between failure and success. Beautiful gardens and outstanding topiary can flourish anywhere, so all aspiring topiary gardeners can be guaranteed success provided they beware the potential pitfalls and design their gardens, train and install their topiary accordingly.

Cold

When hardiness is referred to with reference to plants as a criterion for plant choice, it is usually winter hardiness that is meant. By definition every plant must be hardy somewhere on earth. Some areas never experience significant or prolonged frost while others may be plunged into sub-zero temperatures for many months each year.

In extreme climates, when ground water is frozen, plants cannot replace water lost through transpiration via their leaves and simply shrivel and die. For the purposes of topiary it is usually freezing, drying wind that is most hazardous, as it damages evergreens by 'burning'.

It is not just the basic thermometer reading that has a bearing on plant growth and well-being. In cold weather the damaging aspects of freezing temperatures may be eased by snow cover, for a thick blanket of snow has an insulating effect upon the plants beneath it and may allow some species to survive that would perish if uncovered. Every gardener is delighted to see winter aconites or snowdrops piercing this blanket and high-altitude alpine plants derive every benefit from snow cover.

Levens topiary against trees in the landscape beyond the garden.

Snow scenes at Levens Hall.

Snow scene at Levens Hall.

However, the generally beneficial effects derived from snow cover in the garden are not necessarily good news for topiary. Deep snow on the ground can mean heavy snow on evergreen branches, and weight stress can lead to breaks and damage.

PROTECTING AGAINST SNOW DAMAGE

It is advisable to knock snow off your plant, perhaps using a rake or broom, before the weight of the snow becomes too much to bear. Snow, however, is by its nature self-clearing, and attacking an evergreen tree, especially one topiarized into a prized specimen, with a broom handle requires a lightness of touch or the good intentions of the gardener may end up damaging the plant. So, little and often is always the safest approach when it comes to snow clearing. If you clear it away too soon then the remaining snow may melt and refreeze as ice.

Obviously some topiary forms are more likely to collect snow than others. Tiered fountains and cake-stands as well as flat-topped or animal forms provide broad ledges for deep snow to collect. Where thick snow is a regular feature it is wise to avoid these forms and opt instead for narrow, conical or pointed shapes which will either shed the snow naturally or at least limit its build-up.

On the other hand, particularly in parts of England where snowfalls are unpredictable and often rare and localized, any keen topiarist will want to have a camera ready to photograph the dramatic visual delights of snow on topiary!

With particular reference to box, in view of its extended usage in edging, parterres and knot gardens, the problem of rapid thawing and subsequent refreezing needs to be considered. When quickly warmed by winter sun during the day and then refrozen overnight box can be severely damaged. So it is best to plant box in a part of the garden not subject to this oscillation of temperature, that is, a situation that avoids low winter sunshine. With box it is best to avoid extremes, and even if it remains deeply frozen for the whole winter it is more likely to survive than if it is continually being thawed and refrozen.

Hardiness in plants is variable, with each plant finding its own position on a line between the extremes of heat and cold according to the local conditions. For example, a plant expected to survive a cold winter out of doors could yet fail because the soil is too wet or it is situated in a windy spot. Hardiness is predictable but survival is not, and so it is essential for the topiary gardener to strive for the optimum growing conditions for every plant.

Temporary shelters may of course be erected over or around specimen topiary to protect it from the worst conditions. Like windbreaks, the shelters should be designed to screen and filter the worst weather if possible, rather than be a complete barrier. A breathing mesh or lath shelter is less likely to cause disease problems than an unventilated tent of plastic and less likely to suffer damage itself.

This description of worst-case scenarios requiring desperate remedies is aimed at expanding the climatic range for topiary work. Temporary protection covers are usually quite unsightly and, unless the climate in a particular locality warrants it, are perhaps better avoided. Even then it would become an annual commitment and expense and would have to be balanced with the plant growth.

On the whole topiary is tough and hardy evergreens can survive their customary winter conditions. The above should serve more as a reminder that no garden sleeps through the winter, and that snow and wind can damage artfully pruned topiary in as catastrophic a manner as runaway clipping.

Heat

The opposite extreme from the cold conditions described above is a hot and sunny climate in summer. This is not without problems but it is worth remembering that the two extremes are a vivid depiction of the climate over most of Italy. From a broader range of plant materials some topiary subjects may not respond successfully in hot and sunny conditions. Selecting your plant species with care may avoid this problem but there is still the problem of low rainfall. Artificial irrigation can assist here and is often considered to be an essential part of the infrastructure and is built into gardens in the Mediterranean area. It is axiomatic that a plant that needs watering needs watering for life. Topiary is an art of commitment and response to the climate and seasons and prevailing conditions, which is why it is so appropriate to identify it as the symbol of gardening itself.

Very strong sunshine is not always good news. Some plants may burn in the sun, and scorched evergreens resemble ones damaged in winter by wind chill with their withered and brown foliage. Again, it is vital to use those species that are fully adapted to the prevailing climatic conditions. Even more advantageous is the exploitation of the microclimate of each individual garden. The house itself, trees and other topiary may deliver dappled shade as the sun moves round through the course of the day.

The finished topiary shapes in evergreen can provide a double service in a hot sunny climate. Their endurance as plant material means they are fixtures and of interest even when the last flowers have shrivelled away. They may also be adapted as shade providers in the form of bowers and arbours, shady double-hedge walks and also sunshades. The 'sunshade' at Levens Hall is also, after three centuries of dense growth, impermeable to rainfall. It is for the design of each garden to dictate whether any of these features are necessary to provide shade according to its situation and for the gardener to decide whether they may be included for ornamental purposes only. A bower would be an exciting den for children and could also disguise wheelie-bins in a small garden.

Wind

Wind, too, can cause many problems in the garden. Away from earthquake zones it is the climatic condition most likely to demolish garden features. Topiary that is continually battered and buffeted by the wind is never going to be satisfactory. Although anchored by its roots topiary, even when well established, can be top-heavy and its main stem be under too much stress. Buildings and walls can offer some shelter but solid barriers tend to create localized higher wind-speed turbulence or eddies. In the long term and wherever necessary, shelter-belt plantings outside the garden and hedges within are the answer. They screen and filter air and modify its effect at ground level. Artificial windbreak materials are available that can be used in the short term or at least until shelter belts are established and hedges grow.

Wind not only damages through its physical strength, but also through its cooling and/or drying effect. In some seaside areas it is also laden with damaging salt spray, and seaside areas are of course often windier to begin with. Salt spray is particularly devastating in desiccating the plants it reaches and in stormy weather can travel far inland. Salt-tolerant, seaside-friendly plants need to be chosen to avoid such damage. A coastal zone with damaging, (salt-laden) winds is not the ideal site for specimen topiary. Rounded, (amorphous) forms of a low-lying nature are more likely to succeed.

USING YOUR MICROCLIMATE

No feature of the garden is hardier or more determined than the gardener. Climatic conditions can all be gardened with or guarded against, so should not be a deterrent. Ideal conditions exist nowhere and if they did topiary might require much more than its annual clipping. You just have to be always aware of local conditions. In windy areas low, amorphic topiary sculpture is highly suitable and may be inspired by the natural wind shaping of plants in the locality. In sunny places topiary may provide welcome shade. In cold places evergreens may be the best plant choice. Knowing your own microclimate and garden and its limitations is the way to gain the best results.

THE SOIL

Soil may seem to be another factor over which the gardener has little or limited control, but in fact it can be improved and altered to a considerable extent. The container gardener is able to extend maximum control in this department if using bought-in and prepared growing mediums. When planting specimen topiary, hedges or indeed any permanent tree or shrub material it is essential to get it right from the start, as it is these long-term inhabitants of the garden that will suffer the most if the soil is inadequately prepared. The time and trouble taken in preparation is another investment in the success of the garden as it is difficult to remedy later. With soils, the texture, fertility, pH and drainage are all important.

Texture

Texture describes the physical nature of soils and is directly related to the proportions within it of different-sized particles. An experienced gardener can assess texture by simply taking a handful of soil and feeling it. The ideal loam is geologically a mixture of large sand particles, smaller silt and tiny clay particles, to which a healthy proportion of organic matter gives life. Very few areas are fortunate enough to have such a perfect soil, and generally speaking, something will grow, however badly, in every soil. The soil found in a particular garden can be modified and very much improved through working it and incorporating grit, sharp sand and organic matter as required.

Root-balled tiered specimen being transplanted.

Sandy soils, which crumble in the hand, are too often free-draining so nutrients are quickly leached away, leaving plants hungry. Here the addition of organic matter to add bulk from manure, compost, peat substitutes, leaf mould and surface mulches will help improve the fertility and the moisture-retention qualities of the soil.

Soils with a high clay content, which tend to 'ball' in the hand, are usually poorly drained, sticky and difficult to work. They are impossibly heavy and become completely waterlogged when wet and bake solid when dry. Again the incorporation of bulky organic material improves them immensely, as does the addition of very coarse sharp sand or grit.

The permanent installation of specimen topiary within a garden allows the soil to be improved only once. Annual feeds and mulches are superficial, if beneficial, and do not affect the texture of the soil itself.

In old gardens constant working of the soil may have left its texture as good as it will ever get and topical feeding upon planting may be all that is necessary. Less favoured situations include new housing developments, where the garden may contain very little soil apart from a dressing of topsoil imported as part of the finishing touches of landscaping. There will be very little depth, quality or texture in the soil, and planting stations excavated to a depth of 0.5m and breadth of 1m (1.5×3ft) should be prepared for the better establishment of specimen topiary plants.

Although in time the plant's roots will spread and seek out the nutrients of the unimproved substrate, it is the assistance given over the all-important period of establishment that will kick-start this root search. It also promotes the vigorous growth of the plant, which is the framework from which the topiary work itself will be created.

Giving topiary the best possible start ensures its future success.

Acidity and Alkalinity

The soil's pH and its fertility are interrelated factors that will affect topiary growth. The pH of the soil is a measure of its acidity or alkalinity and is recorded on a scale from 0 (extremely acid) to 14 (extremely alkaline), with 7 being neutral. Soil test kits are widely available, cheap and easy to use and quickly give an instant reading of the soil's pH. A slightly acidic measurement of around 6.5 is often quoted as being the ideal, with the band from 6 to 8 being most appropriate for a wide range of subjects. More extreme readings create problems as they indicate conditions where certain chemicals and nutrients become unavailable to the plants, being locked in either the alkalinity or acidity of the soil.

If the soil is very alkaline (above 8) then this will restrict your choice of plants although in some cases treatment with a chelated or sequestered iron compound may help. Similarly in very acid soil only plants suitable to these conditions are advised unless the ground is treated with crushed limestone or lime.

Organic or ecological policy might encourage gardening with the given soil rather than trying to change it entirely. Soil improvement can only be regarded as responsible gardening in order to optimize results.

Fertility

Fertility, or the availability of nutrients to the plant, in this case topiary, should be thought of as being a long-term need. It is therefore best to encourage a living soil, rich in organic matter which, through natural decomposition, will be the source of slowly released nutrients. Plant growth can also be sustained, of course, through repeated use of artificial fertilizers, but in the topiary garden these are best seen as a supplement.

When planting, if there are doubts regarding soil fertility then it is better to have it tested. The main plant nutrients are nitrogen, phosphorus and potassium (NPK), but a great number of other trace elements are needed. To ensure there is no deficiency the relevant fertilizer must be added and, in view of the long-term demands of topiary, slow-release organic fertilizers are best. Thereafter annual top dressings, early in the season, will boost that year's growth and become ever more important.

An added complication related to plant nutrition is the concentration of chemical salts in the soil. Soluble salts in large doses can burn the roots of plants, especially box, something that is caused very often by an over-zealous application of concentrated fertilizer too close to the plant. Remember the essence of gardening is to feed the soil and let the plant feed itself.

Drainage

Drainage is the last soil-related factor to be considered, but by no means the least important, as it is the factor that governs how much water reaches the roots of the plants and the draining away of excess. Badly drained soil spells death to topiary. Roots are breathing organisms and require air as well as water. To get the right balance there must be air in the spaces between soil particles. Waterlogging of the soil caused by bad drainage will eventually drown the plant.

Bad drainage also leads to the spread of water-borne diseases, which can be devastating; root death quickly leads upwards to entire plant death and in waterlogged soil can pass on rapidly to other specimens in the garden.

If poor drainage is a problem it must be tackled and cured before topiary is planted. Seriously bad drainage may require a piped system of drains. This is beyond the remit of this work and is a problem that may even be best solved by moving house.

Very often, poor drainage is related to soil texture and can be eliminated by soil improvement. Soil compaction, especially on clay soils, is often a feature of vehicle or human traffic and therefore very likely in new housing developments. This produces more or less the same effects as waterlogging. The loss of air at the roots and anaerobic stagnation will soon lead to root disease and death. The one advantage of most new gardens is that they are a blank canvas, often unplanted, and by dealing with soil texture and drainage at the start these problems can be prevented.

Soil compaction can also recur, so it is always important to ensure that pathways lead where people wish to walk and that topiary is not located in the middle of an undesignated walkway or shortcut across a lawn. Deep spiking will open up compacted soil by directing air into the soil and encouraging worms to aerate the soil.

None of the above considerations are discussed to make topiary seem difficult. They are principles of good gardening *per se*. The investment of time, effort and money in creating, establishing and importing and planting specimen topiary is considerable. Therefore it is only sensible to try to get the best out of that investment by ensuring that the plants perform at their best, and the above considerations embrace this desire and concern. If there are problems then to be forewarned is to be forearmed. After all, the effects created are spectacular and well worth the effort. Good gardening practice creates good topiary and furthermore makes for good gardeners.

LIGHT

Topiary grows in the round and so needs light on all sides. All-round, all-over light creates even and tight growth, and topiary specimen plants need to be located where this is available. Topiary is incompatible with shade or shading plants and is not competitive. Potted specimens can be rotated.

Tapered specimen yew obelisk rising from a topiary 'pot' in a walled Dutch garden. The power of the vertical form in gardening is a recurrent theme, all referring back to the image of the Mediterranean cypress growing as an exclamation mark towards the sky. The power of topiary grown in isolation cannot be more greatly emphasized than here.

Contemporary view at Levens Hall showing sculptural juxtaposition of green forms. Light and shade play upon clipped planes and organic growth is turned into creative form.

In reality, except near the equator, most regions will have shady and sunny sides and light variations throughout the year. Localized light levels can vary immensely but the lightest and brightest part of the garden is the situation for topiary. In nature, yew and box may grow in shady or semi-shady woodland, but topiary requires dense and tight all-over growth that is not light-seeking but can remain healthy and contained within the shape it is given. Clipped specimens are also seen to their best advantage in a well-lit situation where the freshness of new growth catches the natural sunlight.

CHAPTER 4

Design: Shapes and Spaces

Topiary in the garden may dominate or be integrated into the overall design. A vast range of inspiration sources both historical and contemporary exist, and with the return to fashion of topiary, suppliers are eager to furnish the practice. Topiary can be bought ready-made and off the peg, can be assisted by netting shapes to be covered or two-dimensional outlines that act as guides, and above all can be seen in other people's gardens. Before looking at a repertoire of shapes and at a selection of suitable plants it is worth looking at the factors to consider when either installing topiary in the garden or creating it oneself. This is not about garden design but rather about the practicalities that affect the choice of an add-on feature to enhance and personalize the garden.

Overview of the topiary garden at Levens.

SHAPE

In deciding on the shape of specimen topiary it is important to remember that although it may be planted in good soil and receive all-round sunlight, the lower parts of any particular specimen will be shaded by the upper parts. Any simple shape needs full light exposure at the base in order to avoid browning off and patchiness. Thus a hemisphere will always work better than a sphere. The principle is that the topiary specimen diminishes in size as it rises.

Topiary naturally grows most vigorously on its upper surfaces and it is these areas that gradually become larger and wider. This is the inherent nature of a tree carrying its spreading crown on top, but will always be at the expense of the areas underneath, which struggle to keep up and whose growth becomes more sparse and straggly as the growth continues. This is actually a gift to the topiarist, as vigorous growth occurs where artistic clipping is most likely to take place. In planning shapes, choosing ones that are wider at the base and have vertical or battered upright surfaces ensures they receive as even a coverage of light as is possible.

NEIGHBOURING PLANTINGS

This refers not only to plants used in association with the topiary as a setting but to the surrounding plants in the garden as a whole. Shading of any kind must be avoided. Overhead shade cast by buildings, trees or even other topiary has been shown to be harmful, for shade equates with less or ultimately no light. Shade can also be created by low plants growing around the topiary itself. If the topiary foliage is to be fit and dense right down to the

Electric clipping of box edging with a sheet down to keep clippings off the gravel.

View at Levens Hall.

ground then care must be taken when planning the area to ensure that whatever is planted nearby, whether annuals, herbaceous perennials, or ground cover plants, does not come too close to the topiary base, thereby cutting out light and causing the thinning and death of lower shoots. Aesthetically this would also damage the look of the topiary specimen, especially in a geometric shape where the base counts as a part of the design profile.

If the overall garden design and perhaps its size requires that plants be grown right up to the base of the topiary, then remember that the bedding of annuals and bulbs as well as herbaceous plants will only create shade for part of the year. On the other hand, planting shrubs, however low, is planting year-round competitors that are far more likely to rob the topiary of light and nutrients.

The roots of any tree can become invasive and damaging, especially in a small garden, so do not forget that topiary is a tree and is no exception. If, for instance, a flower bed is to be placed up against the topiary it is worthwhile creating an underground barrier using a plastic membrane, steel or even stone to prevent the roots choking, starving and drying out the contents of the flower

THE CHILEAN FLAME CREEPER

Many images of topiary show the association of climbing plants with it to soften it and add contrast and extra interest. The best-known plant in this category is *Tropaelum speciosum*, the Chilean flame creeper, with its vivid scarlet flowers that provide a stunning contrast to dark-green yew. It can be extremely difficult to establish, and while not necessarily a good companion plant when over-vigorous, it is a much appreciated familiar. When well established and rampant, however, it can cut out light to the topiary surface – enough to thin, weaken and kill.

Blocks and silhouettes lead the eye towards a golden yew pyramid at Levens. Topiary is an effective eye-catcher, and the golden yew is a reminder that it need not be monochrome.

Sculptural forms are reminiscent of Pharaonic heads. The combination of a battered cube base and rounded crowning headpiece shows multiple-form topiary to perfection.

bed. Established topiary will simply search further afield and not suffer from having to send its roots out away from the flower bed under the barrier. In the same way, topiary planted in a gravelled area with its surface on a membrane can forage under and beyond the barrier in search of sustenance.

ISOLATION AND ACCESS

The need to ensure adequate light on all sides for the topiary has an important corollary – that is, the need to ensure access to all sides of the specimen for other purposes, principally the initial and ongoing training of the tree to its desired shape, but also its regular control and maintenance by annual clipping. Clipping just once a year is usual and generally all that is feasible in a large topiary garden containing many specimens. It is, however, more easily achieved when dealing with clear, geometric shapes than with figurative or amorphous and abstract topiary. Caution and changes may require more frequent attention than one single clipping and easy access is then all the more desirable.

On shapes of up to 2m (6.5ft) in height, access is only needed for the topiarist and his tools. Larger forms are going to necessitate safe, hard standing for ladders, trestles, scaffolding or even hydraulically operated working platforms. Therefore a maximum height of 2m is desirable in single specimens in small gardens where such requirements in infrastructure would alarmingly increase the investment required by the topiary. This also applies, of course, to hedges; it is worth considering and appreciating the amount of work required to maintain major topiary gardens like at Levens Hall.

All-round access for light and maintenance also permits all-round viewing. The viewer can move round to appreciate the shape and form of the living sculpture, enjoy the changes in atmospheric effects on the piece and also select a good vantage point for photography. A single specimen topiary tree in the front of a house might appear to be an obstruction in a photograph of the house rather than the focal point of the lens. From the other

Training a spiral requires attention to detail. This image shows the optimum height of 2m (6.5ft) for topiary without the need for raised access.

side, however, and perhaps seen against a blue sky or distant landscape it becomes the cynosure of attention and the central image of the photograph.

Topiary thrives in isolation. Like all sculpture, whether growing and living or not, it dominates a large amount of privileged space and is a case where less is definitely more. It requires viewing space, room to cast a shadow over the ground and a chance to rise vertically into the sky above. Topiary

Contemporary photograph of topiary garden and hall, Levens Hall.

Summertime view over the garden at Levens Hall.

Historic specimen topiary in full maturity suggesting modern sculpture, a mechanical part or whatever emerged from the mind of its creator.

gardens may seem densely packed but are in fact well spaced out, and the cumulative image is a linking of individual specimens via connecting hedges and edging. There is also an element of topiary speaking unto topiary and as at Levens Hall this dialogue makes a literal conversation piece of the garden wherein different topiary forms can be compared and contrasted, approached from a distance or from a neighbouring specimen. There is a powerful and exciting suggestion here for a neighbouring or even neighbourhood garden concept. Several gardens in a development could each plant a topiary specimen, creating a sophisticated unity and sense of identity – and making a pleasant change from the monotony of bare front lawns.

Traditional, historical topiary gardens were usually meant to be appreciated from a slightly raised position. (Parterres and knot gardens were invariably designed to be seen from first-floor windows – the *piano nobile* of big houses.) Viewing terraces were sited at the north side of the garden to give shelter from north winds. Even now, whether you are planning a large topiary garden or indeed a single specimen, the point from which it is best viewed is an important consideration when it comes to planning the installation.

SIMPLICITY AND THE EFFECTS OF TIME

Most first encounters with topiary are in the form of standard plants. As a method for elevating floral display in fuchsias or for table decorations this is outside the remit of this book, but the classic image of a symmetrically placed pair of standard 'lollipop' bay trees in tubs or pots either side of a front doorway is familiar to all. Invariably the pair would be bought together to ensure uniformity.

It is actually difficult to produce exactly matching pairs in topiary. Two plants may not grow at the same rate and the living, variable material the topiarist is working with may only bend so far to the will. By their very definition geometric shapes require precision and accuracy and only offer an illusion of simplicity.

Rounded, abstract, amorphic and figurative pieces are more easy to get right, quite simply because they are virtually impossible to get wrong. A topiary peacock is only a delightful approximation that is right when there is a cry of recognition and identification. There is always the escape clause that can call it a turkey or dodo.

Simplicity of design is affected by both the scale of the piece and the time available to maintain it. Finely detailed features are quickly lost with fast-growing species and frequent clipping will be required to maintain them. Conversely an over-ambitious piece can be grown out into something less demanding. Over time initial definition will be lost as the plant expands exponentially in all directions. A tight spiral will become more snail-like, for example, more rounded and indeed more

Perspectival vista of form against form at Levens Hall.

A peacock in a pot.

plant-like. As topiary grows it may eventually encroach on paths or block light from other plants, and no amount of hard clipping can maintain it at its original size. Plastic box shapes are the non-growth, lowest maintenance topiary but do not require a topiarist and are the Astroturf of topiary gardening.

The effects of time do enhance the stature, beauty and presence of topiary. The rewards of clipping, good planning and maintenance are immense and the resultant topiary specimen is of long-lasting pleasure to all who enjoy this art form.

CHAPTER 5

Site Preparation and Planting

SITE ASSESSMENT

The first step towards having successful topiary is planning. Time and thought expended at this stage are going to be rewarded by huge savings in time, energy and expenditure later on.

The physical site assessment takes into account its climate, soils, aspect, shading, existing features and domestic services underground.

After this the fun begins as the imagination is called into play. This game is historically called 'absorbing the genius of the place'. Each garden is unique and has a vast range of characteristics that work together to give it this special nature. Few gardeners have the luxury of choosing garden over house, but sometimes it may prove to be its selling point. More often, the garden quite simply comes with the house in the case of the new or is perhaps

Trained box in a nursery.

tired and in need of revitalization in the case of the old. What makes a garden unique can be some part of its content, such as a favourite tree or green lawn; what lies beyond it in a view over a landscape; or the way the sun shines on it and its atmospheric qualities. The genius of the place is more easily read in a historic garden, where the variety and fusion of features and the essence of maturity and continuity forms its personality. In the twenty-first century, the genius of the place is generally the contemporary gardener, whether the owner or an imported designer.

The topiarist needs to look at the garden and assess it with regard to locating topiary specimens. Access was discussed in the previous chapter. Aspect needs to be considered in that the topiary is being installed in order to be viewed and appreciated. It can also be an amenity and screen something undesirable viewed from the house or in fact *make* the view from the house. Its proximity to the house may invite a decking with lights at Christmas or for summer parties. It may stand proud against a sunset.

As for the shape itself, the topiary supplier, pictures of historic gardens or the imagination itself can provide suggestions.

Grander plans are the province of professional garden designers and there is no reason why the hobby topiarist need employ someone else to express his own imagination. The planning is all a part of the pleasure of topiary. Standing in a bare garden with a pen and the back of an envelope to scribble and doodle on is often as far down the line of serious planning and design that needs to be travelled. It has to look right for the gardener both in the imagination and on the ground. The creativity lies in achieving that result.

PLACING THE TOPIARY

An aid to assist the placing of topiary in a garden is to take lots of photographs from the house over the garden or from the garden and outside to the house. A tip is to take a 2m (6.5ft) bamboo cane and include it in each frame; then, when the photographs are printed, draw on them (or place cut-outs of) the intended topiary specimen. Scale is easily maintained by making the rough drawing in felt pen no higher than the cane. This way some options for choice will be created and can be discussed with all who enjoy the garden.

SITE PREPARATION

Various factors are brought into play in the choice of site. As this is an art of display and a subject of great pride and sense of achievement, the site

Variety of shapes in a nursery, in the ground rather than in containers.

A topiary nursery – in Holland as shown by the canal!

chosen is invariably one of prominence and a focus of attention. Topiary is not to be lost in mixed planting but to be exposed to appreciation and enhance its surroundings, making the garden containing it worth a second look for spectators. Once decided, it is up to the topiarist to give the plants the very best start in life there. The quality of the soil is dealt with in the relevant section concerning soil. The specific requirements of the plant species most frequently used for topiary work will be considered below under each plant heading.

To ensure the continuing success of specimen topiary, everything must be done to improve the soil if necessary. It is relatively easy to alter deep soil conditions before planting, but nigh on impossible later on. Essentially a large tree or shrub is being planted, and a cubic metre of soil needs to dug over, and the texture of the soil optimized with the addition of organic material and manure as fertilizer.

Good drainage is just about the most important factor to be considered here. If the drainage is good then that is excellent, if not then adequate drainage must be provided prior to planting or subsequent death of the topiary specimens will be the result. Wide and deep cultivation, incorporating well-rotted organic material, will improve the soil structure and nourish and improve early growth but will not improve drainage; in fact the very act of digging a hole creates an opened-up soil area where water can collect in wet areas. A slightly elevated location in a garden prone to wetness will improve drainage, and incorporating grit and opening up the soil texture will counteract water collection. An elevated position is also prominent and suitable for displaying the topiary specimen. As the topiary grows it will absorb and transpire moisture from the soil like all large shrubs and trees and it is the nature of each successful planting in a garden to optimize the conditions of its situation to its own advantage. Just as successful and healthy shrubs and trees drain away excess moisture, the shade they cast defeats competition for light.

PLANTING

Containerized plants can in theory be planted all year round, but need close attention to their watering requirements if planted during a dry spring or summer. Bare-rooted or root-balled plants are usually planted when dormant. For evergreens the best time would be late autumn or very early spring. The containers or root wrapping should be removed and damaged roots cut back.

In the case of container-grown specimens, tease some roots out of their restricted tight, circular growing pattern. In all cases soak the root ball prior to planting. It is important that plants are not planted too deeply but at the same depth that they were in the pot or nursery bed. Take care to firm them in well, ensuring from the start that there is close contact between the roots and the soil without the planting area being heavily compacted.

Where root systems may have been damaged in transit the main hazard for the new plants will be desiccation until a new root system develops and is thriving. It may be worth considering sheltering new plantings from drying winds if they are exposed and also from strong sunlight. If the root system is significantly damaged, prune away a proportion of the top growth to maintain the requisite equilibrium between root quantity and top growth. At planting, all topiary plants will benefit from a general application of slow-release proprietary fertilizer.

Vertical specimens (especially expensive and ready-trained yew) will require a temporary staking until they are stabilized by new root growth. It is patently obvious that a specimen topiary feature relying on the vertical excitement of its central trunk needs to be precisely vertical and that inserting a stake at a true vertical axis before the initial planting will assist immensely in establishing the desired accuracy at the outset. Plants to be shaped by the topiary gardener will not have much bare stem to guide this procedure, but in training and during aftergrowth the plant will grow upwards to the light (which is another good reason for making certain that light surrounds the topiary). Vertical yew topiary where the bare trunk is intended to be exposed between the layers of, for example, a cake-stand or fountain tiered specimen will look most odd unless the central trunk is absolutely vertical.

Organic and amorphous shapes or those without bare stems and trunks, such as box spheres, cubes, obelisks and pyramids in yew or box, derive the impulse of their form from their subsequent shaping by clipping and do not rely upon initial staking to ensure that the desired shape is ultimately straight and true.

Aftercare

Often, during the first season following transplanting trees and shrubs of all kinds (including topiary specimens), plants will make very little top growth as they are usually and ideally concentrating their efforts on creating new root systems. They are anchoring themselves into the prepared ground and stabilizing their placement. This early root establishment can be enhanced by an annual top dressing of organic fertilizer worked into the surrounding soil. The key indication that this all-important initial establishment has been successful is when new green shoots begin to sprout and emerge from the growth tips of the plant's shoots. With evergreens like box and yew the new foliage is always of a brighter, fresher green and a delightful contrast to the sculptural solidity of the mass of the plant itself.

Pay close attention to ensuring that plants do not dry out during their first season (or for even longer if dry conditions prevail). Bear in mind that even if the surrounding soil is wet it is only when a newly planted shrub succeeds in growing its roots out into it that it can take up the available water. Until then its root system remains the same size as the original root ball. In particularly dry conditions you can apply a mulch using leaf mould, bark chipping, or even well-rotted compost or manure.

Particularly in the early years, competition from other garden plants and weeds should be rigorously discouraged by keeping as large an area as possible around the specimen topiary free from as much plant growth as possible.

Dutch topiary nursery. This topiary supermarket transports its customers down canals rather than aisles.

FORMATIVE PRUNING AND TRAINING

During the first season following planting there will be little new top growth as the shrub establishes itself and produces a viable, expanding new root system.

After this first year you can start to make the first, formative cuts, but you need to have the intended and desired final design in mind. Yew lends itself to vertical growth and the splendours of specimen topiary, tiered and rising above its surroundings and dominating the garden as a distinctive and special feature. It can also be used architecturally as buttresses, obelisks, cubes and pyramids or cones (essentially rounded pyramids). Box is very successful as cones, spheres and hemispheres and also in new topiary work, such as Japanese-inspired cloud topiary. It tends to be used for lower forms than yew. With an initial design in mind the formative stages of topiary work can begin.

The most important thing to establish at this stage is the basic framework of growth from which all the topiary shape's final surfaces will hang. This often means, in practice, choosing a central leader shoot to be the vertical movement and direction of the specimen. This is done by selection and then by elimination of competitors. It may be that half the growth of a plant has to be removed at this stage, but that is fine so long as the remaining material has been carefully chosen to create a fine topiary specimen. This selection of central leader shoots is important for vertical and tiered work of any great height (2m or 6.5ft).

Cutting into a topiary hedge to impart new vigour and light penetration.

That is why it is important to begin with the ideal plant shape in mind, this being wide at the base and tapering towards the top, ensuring that as much light as possible reaches the growing and cut surfaces. Topiary being wider at the base then tapering as it rises is a fixed principle of plant growth and is epitomized in the classic Christmas-tree shape of most conifers.

Whatever the final intended shape of the form, this is the plant outline within which it will be trained and clipped. The strong central leader is all-important to most topiary shapes, and shoots and branches should be allowed to grow out from it at this stage even if ultimately there will be bare trunk revealed. The work at this stage is to strengthen and thicken the main stem. The main stem defines the height of the specimen.

When topiary is fully grown, the aim of the annual clipping is to remove nearly all the new growth from that growing season. This preserves the desired form and allows for a gradual, annual increase in size as the specimen expands. Very young plants waiting to be developed as topiary need a less severe cutting, leaving anything up to half the annual growth.

Once the roots of the newly planted topiary have become established and new top growth has begun to be put on you can start treating the plant as a rather heavily pruned shrub until the desired height or an approximation of the desired shape is arrived at. From this point onwards aftercare is really the combination of creative and artistic pruning, clipping into the desired shape and subsequent annual maintenance clipping.

THE MOST POPULAR FULLY HARDY PLANTS FOR TOPIARY

BUXUS (Box)

Buxus sempervirens
Common Box
Box is the first-choice topiary plant for small-scale work, including low hedges and edging, knot gardens and parterres. There are probably seventy or more species of box found throughout the world, and there are many cultivars available, the most useful being 'Suffruticosa'. It comes with a range of leaf sizes and in gold and silver variegation.

In Britain it grows wild, notably on the chalk of Box Hill in Surrey, but it tolerates a wide range of soil conditions as long as there is adequate drainage. It has been used as topiary material since Roman times, and when you look at the density of its small glossy leaves it is easy to see why. Box is naturally a bushy shrub, which explains the density of its compact foliage. The greatest benefit for the topiary gardener is that the denseness of the foliage is improved by clipping and the small leaves merge to become a single surface.

It is relatively slow-growing and therefore requires only one clipping per year. The disadvantage of this slow growth is that to establish a low hedge or create a knot garden a large number of plants is required as the optimum spacing is 30–40cm (12–16in) apart. Clipping it more than once a year will keep its surface sheen flat and glossy. Creating shapes with box takes advantage of the density of foliage, and severe creative or restorative clipping and shaping should be undertaken in spring before the new season's growth starts. Box roots easily from cuttings taken in early autumn, which actually means that a box edging installed in one bed of a garden could be used to provide plants to edge another after a few years of growth. For the ancient Greeks the evergreen box symbolized the continuity of life, and it most certainly symbolizes the historical continuity of gardening.

ILEX (Holly)

The large spiny leaves of holly do not readily suggest their use in topiary but they do make excellent standard 'mop head' specimen plants and in this form can add a striking note to the centre of a planted area, adding elevated interest. They are very often seen in the hedges of cottage gardens clipped into shape. A careful clipping, or more accurately shapely pruning, with secateurs can create an eye-catching plant for the topiary garden.

Buxus sempervirens.

Ilex aquifolium.

LAURUS (Bay laurel)

Laurus nobilis, the bay laurel, as used in the kitchen, is familiar as the standard in a Versailles tub used as a classic icon of topiary to flank a grand doorway as a pair. Historically it has been trained as mop heads, balls, obelisks, domes and pyramids and makes a striking container plant. Bay laurel is invariably bought-in ready made, but it still requires careful shaping and clipping with secateurs. It can often be found with baroque twisted stems like barley sugar and sometimes woven together as a composite plant of intertwined stems.

Laurus nobilis.

LONICERA (Honeysuckle)

Lonicera nitida, from China, is a tiny-leaved twiggy shrub of this family better known for its scented climbers. It has become popular with topiary gardeners because it is very fast-growing and thus a boon to the creative enthusiast who wishes to sculpt and mould organic and amorphous forms in topiary. It thrives on most soils and does well in shade, which is a great advantage. Its tiny, dark and glossy leaves are reminiscent of box but its growth is less pliable. Constant clipping keeps it dense, otherwise it will soon reach 2m (6.5ft) in height. This is not a costly or difficult plant and is a pleasure to work with as its rapid growth makes its use in green sculpture more akin to working with clay rather than architectural stone. It is problem-free and roots easily. Many topiary artists have taken to this oriental plant with fascinating results (as seen in illustrations in this book).

Lonicera nitida.

ROSMARINUS (Rosemary)

This renowned Mediterranean herb of remembrance has been much used to create aromatic hedges since ancient times. *Rosmarinus officinalis* 'Miss Jessopp's Upright' grows rather more upright, as its cultivar name suggests, and reaches 1.2m (4ft) in height. This is ideal for creating a standard rosemary and a pair of them could be used to create that classical motif of symmetrically flanking a sunny doorway. It would also add solid height to a herb garden containing softer, aromatic plants.

Spectacular topiary menagerie in landscape setting using Lonicera nitida.

Rosmarinus officinalis.

TAXUS (Yew)

The yews contain topiary material of indescribably superb quality. The characteristics which make *Taxus baccata,* common yew, ideal for topiary or hedges are similar to those of box. Yew is slow-growing, which means that it requires less maintenance clipping, but more importantly it retains the crispness of its clipping and shaping for longer. Its tolerance of hard clipping is legendary. It has needle-like leaves, which, when clipped close, create a dense, solid surface of great depth and strength. Its natural growth into a tree means that it has a vertical impetus, which, when trained and shaped, gives all the wonderful benefits of the visual impact of specimen topiary through the ages. This is the most architectural of topiary plants. Like box, yew does not tolerate poorly drained conditions, but otherwise grows in most soil types. The only drawback is the toxicity of the plant, which makes its berries dangerous near children and its foliage undesirable near livestock, although when used as topiary it tends not to produce profuse berries.

Taxus baccata.

The rather deep green and dense foliage of yew responds to light and atmospherics, so while it can shimmer with new growth in the sunlight of early summer on an overcast day it can also absorb all the gloom of a darkened sky. Used as specimen topiary both of these factors are advantages, for when it catches the light it enlivens the garden and enthuses the coloured plants surrounding it. When darkened the drama of its silhouette acts as a strong sculptural presence. Whatever the atmospheric conditions, it provides a perfect foil for surrounding planting with brighter, more cheery colours. It is the topiary star for historic gardens and is equally valuable in a smaller environment, where a single specimen can add a symbol of pride and success to the amateur topiarist's garden.

Because it is slow-growing it really only needs one annual clipping in midsummer. Training and shaping take place in spring.

Yew has to be the most instantly recognizable specimen topiary plant, and is familiar throughout Britain as the churchyard tree. Shaped and clipped to immaculate precision it is the symbol of the historic topiary garden in England.

The above list is not intended to be comprehensive, for like all arts and crafts, topiary has embraced other materials and plant species. These are the 'classic' plants and the ones this book is based on, mainly because they are so successful and partly because they represent the mainstream of topiary tradition in gardening.

CHAPTER 6

Clipping

THEORY

When trees and shrubs are allowed to grow naturally, without intervention from shears or clippers, they form a distinctive natural shape. This may be modified by poor growing conditions caused by soil variations, geology or climate – wind is a tremendous natural tree shaper. There is endless variety in nature and sometimes it is only in captivity, when trees are nurtured in isolated splendour under optimum conditions in a botanic garden or arboretum, that the ideal or textbook shape is attained. The beauty of this variety and the soaring growth of trees into areas of sky where the silhouettes of distinctive and individual crowns are noticeable is not what is required in topiary. This is where topiary differs from bonsai culture, which strives to reproduce in miniature the natural form of the mature tree.

The sculptural art of topiary is the aesthetic department of the growth control practice of pruning. The desired result is a particular shape and in order to maintain this shape the extent of annual growth is controlled as a matter of maintenance. During the period of years over which the chosen tree species is grown and trained into the desired shape, growth is encouraged but severely controlled. After that the shape may continue to increase in dimensions but is maintained by annual clipping. Apart from shape, the second desired effect in topiary is a smooth and even close finish on the exterior, which is achieved by increasing the surface density of the foliage, hopefully sustained by a relatively rigid structure underneath. All this requires a careful maintenance programme of clipping operations, which is the principal physical intervention undertaken in this art form.

The tools of the trade.

New growth on box effectively disguising its cone shape. This is to all intents and purposes the natural plant shape, and the topiary cone lying within has to be recovered by clipping with hand shears.

THE UNDERLYING SCIENCE

In order to understand topiary it makes sense to investigate what makes a plant tolerate constant, annual clipping and how it can be persuaded to co-operate in the art of topiary. In normal growth conditions – where soil, moisture, climate and nutrients are available freely – the apical or end shoots of the plant produce growth hormones which suppress growth from side buds below them. In other words, vertical growth is favoured over horizontal. Wherever there is a leaf joining the main vertical stem, at its leaf axils, a bud can be found resting which has the potential to develop into a new shoot if conditions are favourable. Most of the time, though, these buds remain dormant, as all energy is directed into the extension growth at the tip of the main shoot.

In unclipped trees and shrubs at the end of the growing season, shoots produce what are called terminal resting buds, which overwinter as punctuation marks. In spring they will break into growth and continue into development as a further, single, long extension shoot. You can see this most clearly in single-stemmed young plants growing in nursery conditions. Further back along the growing leader the effect of its hormonal activity will begin to diminish and side shoots will develop.

By clipping, trimming, pruning, or removing the terminal bud in any way, the hormonal messengers are sent back to the suppressed axillary buds. The result is a great multiplication of side growths at

Scaffold platform work above 2m (6.5ft).

lower level. This is why, when you buy windowsill plants in pots you are generally advised to pinch out the tips to make them bushy.

Repeated trimming continues to remove all new apical buds and thus further lateral growth is encouraged to fill out the plant and increase its density. This is enhanced by cutting back each time to the same plane, or almost, resulting in a surface of very densely packed growth. This is the ultimate tight, close-textured, leafy surface desired for topiary sculptures. Apart from the leaves and some of the main trunk, all structural parts of the plant – branches and twigs – are in effect hidden behind this surface growth.

TIMING

This is one area that gardeners are always debating, and not just with regard to clipping topiary. For each plant there may indeed be an optimum time for each operation but for each gardener, amateur more so than professional, this has to be balanced with the time available. Practically every gardening operation can equally well be attempted on an opportunistic basis. Correct or textbook timings, advice from magazines, newspapers and television and radio programmes certainly act as guidelines and can be guaranteed to refer to the most suitable quarter of the year, or month even. In real life, however, where most amateur gardeners are weekend gardeners with many other demands on their lives, then the best time to do the job is when opportunity, inspiration, enthusiasm and the weather all conspire to make it possible.

So clipping has its periods in broad outlines as explained below. With most species used for topiary and in most climatic zones, there are definite seasons of growth (spring and summer) and definite dormant seasons (autumn and winter). Aesthetically, the best time to appreciate the shapes and forms of topiary is when they are trimmed back to the tight lines of their designated designs – that is, they look at their best just after being clipped and before fresh, new, green growth blurs their crisp outlines once more.

Timing of their annual trim can thus be determined to maintain the pieces at their optimum sharpness of outline for the longest period by removing the new growth at the end of the growing season. This is the technique used most often in large, historic topiary gardens, where for many practical and economical reasons it is only possible to do a maintenance cut of each piece once a year.

Detailed hand clipping at Levens Hall.

In the conditions prevailing in the UK most clipping work is undertaken in late summer. This gives the longest period of time – right through until the following summer months of May and June – in which to enjoy the tightly clipped shapes.

The organization of labour throughout the year in a large topiary garden with many other demands on the gardeners' time and skills is a completely different story from that of the private individual. When labour exceeds work then it can be utilized more frequently and intensively. Where perfect results are desirable at all times and when topiary is still in its formative stages then clipping more than once a year will provide the best results. Specimen topiary in small gardens will be expected to look its best all through the summer months, and if you have a single splendid example as the centrepiece of a garden then you will be continually fine-tuning its look in order to maximize its display value. Extra clipping is also necessary where you are using a species with a vigorous growth habit, which will end up with continually blurring outlines if left unattended. Vagaries of climate and variations in the weather pattern may also cause excess growth, or alternatively impede it, and the clipping work can be adjusted accordingly. It will be understandably difficult for the amateur topiary enthusiast to ignore a specimen of green sculpture situated in the centre of a lawn which is cut very regularly throughout the growing season. Light snipping to fine-tune the work of topiary art may be carried out monthly, and once the effect of this upon the surface finish and the silhouette of the outline is noticed then it will become part of its maintenance regime. New pieces tend to invite frequent attention as if delivering an incentive to grow.

WHEN TO AVOID CLIPPING

Times when not to clip are prescribed first and foremost by adverse weather conditions. In the UK in particular, cold and frosty conditions are not conducive to the trim. Box, one of the mainstays of the historic topiary tradition, can be severely damaged if cut during icy periods. With this plant it is traditional to trim only after the last possibility of night radiation frost has passed, which is normally at the end of May or beginning of June. Any new growth made thereafter will have time to harden off sufficiently before cold conditions return in the following winter.

At Levens Hall the clipping takes place through the autumn and into the early winter, which slightly bends the rules. This has to do with staff availability

The team at work at Levens.

and has rarely caused any more than minor damage, invariably box being scorched after cutting in particularly frosty conditions.

Clipping box too early is a mistake. Fine spring weather can incite gardeners to many inappropriate garden activities, which they will rue when good weather in April is followed up by frost which kills or severely damages fresh new growth. Fine weather after late clipping can also induce fresh new growth to be later damaged by frost. Old and established box growth is, of course, almost totally hardy, certainly in the majority of varieties and species available in the marketplace.

Yew, that other great mainstay of the topiary tradition, can also be clipped more than once a year for a tighter, more controlled result. The first big flush of new growth in spring can be clipped in July. Later on in September a second and tidying trim of any new shoots can be undertaken. If only one cut is possible then it is advisable to wait until after August but before the onset of the worst winter weather.

The preference overall is for early cutting. *Lonicera nitida* and privet (*Ligustrum*) are extremely vigorous growers that lend themselves to rapid hedge growth and fast topiary work. While as hedges they can rapidly become unkempt unless cut frequently, the need for frequent cutting renders them highly plastic green material for topiary as they invite, if not demand, frequent clipping.

Beech (*Fagus sylvatica*) and hornbeam (*Carpinus betulus*) are two stellar hedging plants requiring only one trim per year. Although deciduous trees, as hedging plants they retain their foliage throughout the winter in its autumn colouring and although not usually considered to be specimen topiary material make excellent architectural hedging.

Holly (*Ilex aquifolium*) and other large-leaved evergreens are often trimmed in late spring and perhaps once more in late summer. These species, like the bay laurel of the doorstep, are best tackled with secateurs, removing entire leaves, as leaves cut across will brown, wither and look unsightly. The time this takes is justified by the results but may well be a factor in determining whether such plants are chosen as topiary specimens in the first place.

TOOLS

There is a range of tools available for topiary training and trimming. Your choice of tool is usually governed by the amount of work involved, its size and extent, and of course the funds available.

Topiary gardener at work.

Topiary is all about cutting and clipping, so one of the most important points to constantly bear in mind with any tool is the maintenance of the sharpness of the cutting edge. Topiary requires a certain precision and the flat planes and sharp silhouettes of its subjects need a clean and sharp cutting. The clipping art of topiary can only be practised with razor-sharp cutting tools. When the tools selected are brand new they are very sharp and will all function extremely well. Inevitably they will lose the sharpness of their edge over time and how well they continue to perform will depend on the care taken by the user in looking after and maintaining them. One could, quite appropriately, quote the old saying that a 'craftsman is only as good as his tools'. An unsuccessful craftsman will always blame his tools or perhaps even worse not realize that the effectiveness of his clipping has been diminished by the substandard maintenance of his tools. To be fair, topiary specimens that need clipping just once a year may easily cause the tools used to languish neglected during the rest of the year.

All clippers come with full manufacturer's operating and safety instructions, and these should of course be studied and followed closely at all times. Because they are intended to be comprehensive they may look complicated. Safety is a top priority in the garden and applies as much to the amateur, hobby topiarist as to the professional gardener looking after a collection of historic specimen topiary. Obviously the more work is to be undertaken the more rigorous the safety procedures must be.

Gloves should be worn at all times when using sharp or mechanical tools. They are the front-line defence and need to be chosen to fit comfortably and grip well. They also need to be tougher than gloves designed to keep the hands clean while in the garden. Eye protection and ear defenders may also be necessary.

Professionals would usually wear a chainsaw operator's helmet, which has a mesh visor, to stop any flying plant debris from hitting the face, most especially the eyes. Unlike glasses, goggles or clear plastic visors they do not get steamed up or smeared. They have ear defenders built in, and the helmet prevents damage to the head. Most usefully they also have a small cape at the back for protection in heavy rain.

Secateurs

Regarded as an essential tool by any gardener, a good-quality pair of secateurs is an indispensable part of the topiarist's battery of tools. They are, of course, very much used in the formative stages of topiary development, but are also essential for continuing maintenance. Indeed, large-leaved evergreens like holly and bay laurel may need to be trimmed by secateurs alone in order to preserve the entirety of the leaf size.

Very fine detail is often better trimmed using secateurs or sheep shears for their precision.

Using secateurs to incise definition into a topiary piece.

Likewise, individual stray shoots or sucker growth is best removed with a snip of the secateurs.

Secateurs are small and portable and can be fitted into a holster attached to the belt so they can travel around the garden aboard the gardener and be extracted for use whenever an opportunity is seen. They fit directly into the hand and operate as ergonomically as you could wish as an extension of the hand, functioning like the scissoring action of the index and middle fingers. Whichever brand you go for, the important thing is to choose them by holding them and feeling them. The weight, balance and ease of unlocking the closed blades are all important. How important easy maintenance and sharpening are depends upon the mileage required from them. It is perfectly possible to spend little and rebuy frequently, but gardeners tend to become fond of their tools, and a good pair, which is one that feels good in the hand and works easily without necessarily being expensive, rapidly becomes a favourite tool. Be warned: their effectiveness at cutting plant material should not tempt you to cut wire or wood with them, as this will stress and damage them.

Tribute to the topiary gardener. Hand clippers are always the best.

Hand Shears

In terms of control and result, hand shears are surely the mainstay of any topiarist's tool kit. They have been the traditional clipping tool for centuries and their family tree includes sheep shears and textile equipment among the ancestors. Their principle is the meeting of opposing blades under pressure from the controlling hands, which delivers force and cut at the same time. If secateurs are an extension of the hand then shears unite both arms in a single delivery of purpose. They are simple in operation and contain few moving parts. Although little can go wrong, looking after them properly will ensure that they have a long life.

Different models do have different features, and at this point it is as well to examine these, remembering that it is the initial handling prior to purchase that most often dictates the choice made by the gardener and topiarist.

Blades

Firstly the working end of the tool needs to be considered, and this is of course the blades. Usually both blades will have sharpened cutting edges ground onto them, but this is not always the case. Certain shears have one flat striking edge like an anvil and one opposing cutting edge. The great advantage of this type of shears is that the plant growth, particularly when soft, cannot slide between two opposing blades and be squashed and folded but is effectively caught against the surface blade and cleanly cut by the opposing sharpened edge.

Some blades are straight along their length while others can be wavy along their cutting edge or even notched at the base. The idea behind these designs is that larger and tougher growths are not just squeezed under pressure or pushed up and out of the blades, but are caught and held immobile until the cut is delivered. This is a very useful feature for the topiarist.

All opposing blades only ever deliver a cut at the point where they make contact and meet. This is important for ease of use as it avoids friction, and the hard work necessarily involved in using them is kept to a minimum.

The securing bolts that join the opposing sides of the shears should ideally be removable to make maintenance easier. They should also be adjustable so that you can tighten or slacken the action of the opposing blades.

Handles

With regard to the handles, how comfortable they are to hold depends in the first instance on the presence of rubber shock-absorbing stops on their upper parts. Comfort during the use of the shears is greatly improved by their presence because the jarring transferred up through the joints of the arms every time the shears snap closed is reduced.

Lastly, to the handles themselves. These may be of wood, plastic or rubber composite. Wooden handles are often either painted or varnished when new but it is a good idea to sandpaper this attractive outer coating back into the smoothness of the natural wood. Returning to the solid material of the tool and thereby eliminating surface smoothness creates a better relationship between hands and tool, improves the feel of the tool and also reminds one of the craftsmanship that has gone into making traditional hand tools. Sandpapering will also improve the grip on hard plastic handles.

It is the grip and feel of hand-held tools that is ultimately so important and governs their effectiveness in use. Garden tools act as extensions of the arm and hand; where there is no natural adhesion or friction even between hand and tool, the grip needs to be tighter and focus and concentration are on the handles rather than the cutting edge. Professionals tell of fatigue and hand cramps after extended use of tools that are not ideal. For amateurs they recommend creating an easier grip on shears by sanding the wooden surface. What may cause stress and fatigue in professionals who are constantly using the tools is in fact much worse for occasional users who do not possess compensatory reflexes. Like most tools made of wood, the handles of shears fare better when slightly damp. Craftsmen of old would spit on their hands before taking wooden tools into their grip.

Grip improvement can also be brought about by treating the shears handle rather like a tennis racket and winding adhesive tape, available from sports suppliers, around the handles. This will not only improve the grip but also act as a shock absorber.

Finally, the last recommendation is to use lightweight gripper gloves. The unprotected hand is a risk area when gardening, and safety is an essential consideration when out in the garden. The ungloved hand is not only unprotected from thorns and other sharp edges but is also smooth and thus not the most effective gripping implement. Gripper gloves are sold to the building industry and other workers who lift and shift; their gardening excellence is that they reduce fatigue when working by reducing the hand pressure required to keep a tool correctly positioned in the hand.

METAL FOR SHEARS

New shears are all sharp but they become blunt through use. Some chrome-hardened materials stay sharp longer, but pay for that by being difficult to resharpen. There is a lot to be said for the use of plainer steel, which can go rusty if left out in the rain and does lose its cutting edge relatively quickly. The advantage is that it can easily be sharpened to razor precision and become once more the finest cutting edge the topiarist could use when shearing specimen topiary. For an occasional amateur topiarist, steel-bladed shears may well be the best choice, as they can be put away for the winter, brought out and sharpened and be as good as new.

Safety

Bear in mind that a good set of shears is a very sharp tool and the clipper's hands need to be kept well away from the blades – wear gloves as advised above. When not in use, the tool must be stored out of reach of children.

Maintenance

Hand shears with their long blades can be sharpened using small, pocket-sized diamond-surfaced files. The same rules about keeping them clean and lubricated apply as for clippers. Sharpening is an ongoing practice with professional gardeners, as it is only common sense to keep the blades sharp at all times rather than wearing them down to a state of bluntness before taking action. Spraying with water also facilitates use.

A good way of testing the cutting condition of a pair of shears is to try them on a sheet of paper: a clean cut along the length of paper means the tool is in optimum condition, otherwise sharpening is needed.

For sharpening, wear gloves and use a small diamond-faced flat file. These last much longer than metal files and deliver a sharpening rasp to the blade while being light to the touch. It is important to hold the shears steady for this task and a vice is ideal for this purpose. Obviously the sharpening needs to follow the angle of previous sharpening and only that side should be operated on. When finished, quickly passing the file along the opposite side will remove any burr on that side by turning it back.

A more thorough removal of the burr or roughness that builds up at the very edge of the sharpened blade can be undertaken using a butcher's steel. This, when rubbed along the length of the edge at the same angle as the file was used, will eventually weaken and rub off the burr, leaving a razor-sharp cutting edge. Any filings that remain should be simply washed off with water.

It is possible to have most garden shears sharpened professionally.

Electric Clippers

Moving up the scale to electric clippers is worth considering when facing work of greater extent. These hedge clippers (as they are designated) all operate on a similar principle. They contain reciprocating blades of varying lengths driven by a motor. Electric hedge trimmers are most definitely the most popular and are available in garden centres and DIY stores from many manufacturers and to many specifications.

With all mechanical clippers, weight and balance are of prime importance. Tools used for extended periods of work must not be heavy or awkward to hold, and even tools used infrequently need to be comfortable to handle.

Both single-sided and double-sided blades are available. Single-sided blades do not have the disadvantages they might at first suggest. The ensuing slight reduction in weight allows for a slightly longer blade and all other things being equal they are just as effective in use.

For intricate work using the long edge of the electrical trimmer, a shorter blade is a definite advantage. This applies to sculpturally complex topiary. For larger pieces and hedges the longest blade, wielded in a swathing action, will be the

Sharpening hand shears.

Using electric clippers with a safety helmet with a cape, and with the cable carefully fed through a belt loop.

optimum choice. It is far easier to create smooth, flat planes using a long tool in broad sweeps than nibbling away with short clippers.

Small clippers powered by rechargeable batteries are also available, but they will always be limited by their battery life and may need to be recharged more than once a day if lengthy work is undertaken. Some models come with a battery pack that is fitted to the waist or even mounted on a backpack and attached to the clippers by a short length of cable. These are extremely useful and convenient tools to have in one's armoury and are particularly handy for more limited or lightweight tasks.

On many mechanical clippers produced in recent years the rear handle can be rotated through 180 degrees. On long stretches of hedging where the operator is working along one plane in a single direction this can be extremely useful. But under normal circumstances it is always better to leave the handle in the standard position as this lets you make cuts in all directions.

Safety

The UK mains voltage is 240 volts a.c. and this can easily kill. This explains why electrical hedge trimmers usually incorporate lots of safety features, but even so they are never advocated for use under wet conditions. They should always be used in conjunction with an RCD circuit breaker (readily available from DIY stores), which will cut off the mains supply almost instantly if a fault occurs. Increasingly in this type of tool, micro-switches are incorporated into each handle (the two points you grasp) so that they can only be operated when both hands are firmly in place around both handles and therefore, most importantly, away from the blades. Fast 0.1-second blade brakes are another feature to look for: this feature will stop the blades moving the instant either of the handle switches is released.

A flex that is a bright, visible orange or yellow is easier to avoid cutting through. It is also a good idea to keep the flex behind you, by simply throwing it over your shoulder or by attaching the lead to a karabiner on the back of your belt. The operator of electric clippers needs to be aware of his position in relation to the flex at all times and should ensure it is out of danger of being cut by the working end of the tool.

In general terms, the more modern the hedge trimmer the more safety features it will incorporate, but the cutting edge of the blades can still cut the human body and indeed plants not requiring treatment, so control needs to be rigid at all times.

Wear suitable protective gloves to improve your grip, as well as eye protection – goggles are readily available from DIY stores. For prolonged clipping using a noisy electrical trimmer, ear defenders are essential, but if working on a single specimen in a small garden the relatively short amount of time involved in the job may not make that quite so imperative.

Maintenance

The smooth operation of all clippers relies on lubrication. Manufacturers will indicate the points where lubrication, in the form of oil or grease, needs to be applied, but it also vital to keep the cutting edges clean and lubricated during use. Light spray oils, such as WD40, can be used occasionally during the working day or every time the clippers are used in the domestic garden. Excessive use is costly, and contact with plant material in excess can be damaging. Some professionals would advise repeated spraying with plain water from a hand-held spray pump as this not only keeps the blades clean and lubricated but removes any build-up of sap and green plant gums, which would otherwise slow the clippers and make them harder to work with. Any build-up of material on the cutting blades forces them apart slightly and prevents a sharp, clean cut; this spoils the finished effect as leaves are stripped rather than cut and twigs are chewed rather than snipped clear. This poor finish is referred to in some professional circles as the 'candle effect', presumably because of the knobbly surface created.

After use, hose off the clippers (detached from a live power source) at the cutting end where the blade teeth are to keep them clean, and then spray with a lubricating oil. This is essential if you use the clippers frequently, but is also extremely important in a domestic setting if the clippers may be put away and not used for some time.

For the sharpening and the set of the clippers it is prudent to follow the manufacturer's advice and heed their guidelines and instructions. Professionals will have their tools serviced, sharpened and reset once a year before the start of the cutting season. Of course all tools' operational life and need for attention is affected by any abuse, whether accidental or not. It goes without saying that if you try cutting larger branches or cut into soil filled with blunting stones, then the tools will suffer.

Sharpening clippers is not too technical a task but is time-consuming if done correctly. There are a lot of teeth on mechanical clippers to be attended to. The best result is achieved by slow hand filing (after cleaning and drying). Faster power grinders will overheat and soften the tempered metal.

The set of the blades is also crucially important. Reciprocating blades must run as tightly together as possible without being slowed down by frictional contact. Manufacturers offer guidelines, but with familiarity and frequent use, trial and error is often the best method.

It is always possible to have power tools serviced professionally; the choice really depends on how confident you feel doing it and the time you have available.

Petrol Clippers

These mechanical tools are the real heavyweight clipping tools. They usually pack more power than their electrical equivalents and can cut into thicker plant material and even branches. This is only really of value, however, if more than the current year's work is being dealt with at one time. This rarely occurs in topiary and hedge work except in restoration projects, where sadly and heavily overgrown material is being reclaimed from the wild.

Using a petrol clipper on a box.

Restoring the sloping planes to a topiary pyramid using a stick for straight edge guidance and clearing away clippings.

They do have the significant advantages that there are no trailing wires, they are not dependent on a mains electricity supply point or electrical generator and most usefully of all can be used in wet conditions without risk of electric shock. They are powered by small, two-stroke engines running on a petrol/oil mixture. Their main disadvantage is that the operator unfortunately but inevitably inhales exhaust fumes, so wearing a face mask is advisable. They are also quite heavy to use and the noise levels produced are high so may raise objections from neighbours and scare livestock and wildlife. You also need to have a secure storage place for the flammable fuel.

Despite all this, petrol clippers are very useful to professional gardeners and in their heavier versions have agricultural applications. These are tools for those intending to undertake large-scale topiary and hedge work at a professional level and for freelance gardeners travelling round to various work places, since the autonomous source of power means they are not dependent on having access to property. Maintenance is as for electric clippers (*see* above).

Long-Reach Hedge Trimmers

Another quite recent development has been the long-reach hedge trimmer. These are basically strimmer engines attached to longer handles with an adjustable trimmer attachment fitted to the other, working end. These tools essentially extend the reach of standard clippers without necessitating climbing ladders. They also give a close shave to flat planes, enhancing the finished appearance.

Using extended clippers to reach further.

The disadvantage of this invaluable tool is that the extra physical effort required to hold its length in position tires the operator very quickly, so it can only be used for short spells of work. For short-term use they are a valuable additional tool but do not constitute a replacement for standard clippers. Again, for the sake of safety, strong gloves and eye and ear protection are advised when using any mechanical tools.

Pneumatic and Hydraulic Clippers

Pneumatic and hydraulic clippers have been developed for specialist fields. They are still really at the development stage and to date none match the efficiency of the electrical or petrol versions, and so can be discounted here.

GARDEN CANE

A thin stick or garden cane used to flick away the clippings from the surfaces is a cheap but indispensable tool of the trade. Its length depends on the size of the topiary specimen being clipped. A refinement of this might be to attach several thin twigs to a longer, thicker stick, thereby creating a simple switch or besom. These are effective in use and nothing commercially available quite matches them.

Long canes also provide a straight edge to act as guideline when clipping. They help the eye to measure up the job and can act as rough and ready measuring sticks for comparison and confirmation.

Working from the top down.

CLIPPING TECHNIQUE

This section covers the approaches to and the actual methods employed in giving topiary pieces their regular trim.

Topiary, as living sculpture, is unlike any other art form in that it can never be called finished. There is no final end product as such, for unless it is regularly maintained and disciplined it will change beyond all recognition and revert back to the green material from which it was created. Topiary is a process, a continuing journey, rather than a destination.

Of course the very act of planting, training and shaping a piece of specimen topiary requires the topiarist to have an intended form firmly in mind. This is the end to strive for and is assisted by every clipping. But it must be remembered that we are attempting to control and manipulate nature, and natural forces have a habit of resisting such interventions and regaining control. Branches may sag, growth may thin and die or be too strong or dominant elsewhere, and shoots may appear where they are not desired.

Plants grow, expand and develop and their character changes with time. Most trees live much longer than the allotted span of the gardener. Where a tree may be fully mature only after a century or even longer, the topiarist is actually trying to create something mature and finished in a relatively short space of time; the topiarist can use this to his advantage by starting with an appropriate end result in mind.

The annual, natural cycle of growth means that however sharply and clearly topiary is cut it will only be a matter of time before the definition thus acquired will lose its sharpness and become blurred. In other words, the topiary will require cutting once more.

When attempting to clip a mature or shaped piece of topiary it is important to study it in the round. Whether it is geometrical, representational, stylized or abstract it will possess an ideal form, and it has to be returned to that shape. Ideally all vertical planes should be vertical and right angles precise where they occur. Spheres, cubes, cones and pyramids have the precision of their symmetry to be maintained. Birds and animals have their proportions to be respected with heads and tails of an acceptable size. Abstract work has to appear abstract rather than a botched attempt at something more precise or geometrical. Unfortunately, if a peacock loses its head it does not automatically become convincingly abstract.

It is not necessary to reach absolute perfection in one first attempt. Gently coaxing and nudging the shape in the right direction counterbalances the force of nature moving in the opposite direction. This co-operation with nature acts in the favour of the topiary, which each year grows better and stronger giving more material to work with and improving upon the quality of the work.

Method

Clipping topiary is a bit like hairdressing – every piece is an individual case but there are still general principles to be applied.

It is usual to start at the top and work down. This allows the clippings to be removed or flicked away as work proceeds and is a more sensible approach for the good of the piece, as each completed section can be viewed from below as work continues downwards. Plants naturally grow strongest and thickest at the top and it is therefore possible to clip hard back in this area before moving down to more shaded and less dense growth. Following the line from the top, much less needs to be clipped off the lower areas in order to maintain the integrity of the shape. Starting from the bottom could tempt you towards cutting back harder than necessary where it was not needed, and eating away into softer growth lower down would not guarantee a continuation of the line to the top. In simple geometric shapes this would create overhanging verticals, and the result would be highly unsuccessful and difficult to remedy. In figurative or tiered work you would end up with top-heavy pieces that perhaps look unstable and tottery.

As for the act of clipping itself, there should be an imaginary line of perfection towards which the clipper aspires and directs the operation. Rather than cut back to that line in one clipping it is better to make a number of passes with the cutting tool. First of all, roughly cut away about 75 per cent of the growth to take off the toughest growth. On yew in particular it is noticeable that there are

Tools, access structure and finished work.

usually two distinct layers or flushes of growth. You will find long shoots of about 15cm (6in), with at their bases a 5cm (2in)-thick infilling growth between the shoots. It is this longer layer of growth that is taken off with the first swipe of the clippers and this gives you a much clearer picture of the shape beneath.

On established pieces in good condition you should aim for the clipping to return the shape back to the level of the previous year's cut, certainly to within 5mm (0.2in). Cutting all growth off is not a good idea with regard to the well-being of the plant. Some fresh foliage is needed to sustain its ongoing life processes, and furthermore the fresh growth of the next season depends upon buds lying dormant under this season's layer. The topiarist must always respect his subject as a living, growing plant and not just regard it as a piece of art.

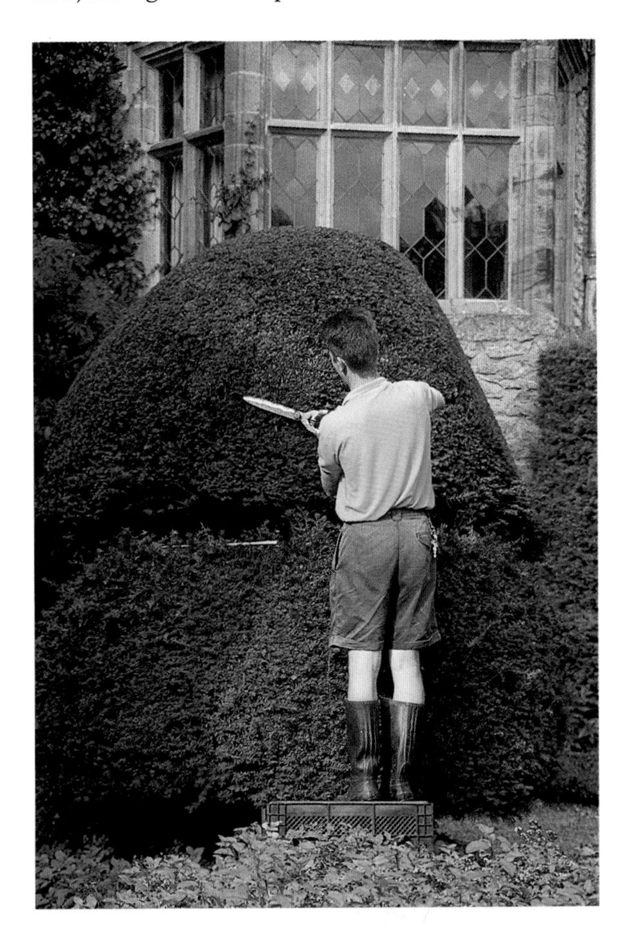

Standing on a box makes all the difference.

There remain the final few centimetres of growth to be removed by trimming, and this is cleaned away by several passes of the blades. Removing the clipped-off trimmings as work proceeds makes it possible to assess the success of the cutting, so use the cane constantly to flick away debris – this also raises hidden shoots tucked away so that they do not escape the clipping. Most importantly, step back frequently to admire the work in progress and to look at it from more than one viewpoint, so you can assess which parts require further clipping; this will also help you build up confidence. Unfortunately clipping is close-up work so the eye is only a reliable assistant at a distance. The finished result depends on this constant checking and assessment. In between clips spray the blades with water to keep them running freely.

Whatever is being clipped, this constant standing back and assessing the work so far is all important. It is especially effective when flat planes can be compared with other flat planes in an effort to ensure that they are as horizontal as possible. Vertical lines can be compared with the house or a cane stuck in the ground. The best way to view topiary and assess it is against a clear and uncluttered background such as the sky. On rounder and more figurative shapes there is little to guide the topiarist other than memory and familiarity with the shape, so working out where to cut to is a matter of skill and judgement. When the shape is more geometric and straight-sided there are certain guides to assist.

Very occasionally a plumbline may be used as well as the cane. This can be any heavy stone or object attached to a length of string and dropped to indicate a vertical. You can also use more ambitious framework systems but they are more likely to impede clipping than assist it. Wire and mesh frames and outlines for small-scale figurative work are recommended for that specific category of topiary and are extremely popular as fun and festive topiary aids. Larger work requires imagination and the confidence in your ability to implement what you see in your mind's eye. With the finished green sculpture in mind the clipping can go ahead.

On some specimens the line is far easier to see because of the variation in colour of the foliage from the previous year to the current one. Variegated or golden topiary in particular exhibits this

Planks and trestles used for access at Levens Hall.

characteristic. The previous year's leaves turn darker green while the fresh new growth is a brighter, more yellow green. Similarly, cutting earlier rather than later will ensure a physical difference in the appearance of the growth, as the current year's growth will still be soft, fresh and possibly lighter in colour. The line to be cut to can also be discerned from working down to where the previous year's cut leaves and twig ends are discovered, there being usually a denser surface on established specimens. Yew notoriously can throw up competitive upright shoots towards the sides of the pieces (rather like rose suckers), and these should be removed as quickly as possible.

When it comes to achieving the smooth velvet finish of newly clipped topiary, the secret is to sweep the clippers across the surface in many different directions. Topiary clipping requires a certain boldness of action, and nibbling away rather than shaving the surface in the manner of a scythe will only result in a pock-marked surface.

Professional gardeners work in all weather conditions. For the topiarist, different weather brings different advantages and disadvantages. Wet weather would exclude the use of electrical clippers but ensures that shears stay clean and sharp. Bright sunshine is often a time to be out in the garden but can, especially when the sun is low in the sky, impede the clipping work by dazzling the clipper. Windy conditions obviously make any work at a height impossible, and can also animate the topiary piece, making it impossible to cut as it blows around. Still, for topiary that requires a single annual clipping it is not going to be impossible to find an ideal day within the optimum time period for the carrying out the operation.

Clearing Up

With a little foresight, clearing up can be made fairly easy. If the topiary is growing amid other plants then you can simply brush the clippings off the surrounding plants and leave them on the ground as a mulch. However, if the clippings are going to be visible and potentially unsightly evidence of your activity then they need to be removed. This is where spreading of some form of sheeting underneath the specimen will make life easier. You can also rake up the clippings with a spring-tined rake, although this will remove only larger growth. If every leaf needs to be removed and tidied away then the best solution is to blow them away with a garden vac. These are very popular with gardeners who have to deal with annual autumn leaf fall, and they are used at Levens Hall to swiftly clear away the tiny box clippings from pathways, leaving the gravel looking clear and clean.

ACCESS

Since most amateur topiarists will create pieces only up to 2m (6.5ft) high or thereabouts, problems of access do not really exist. With historic topiary gardens, where centuries of growth have created gigantic specimens, aids to access are required; these are usually never seen by the visitor which is why they will be outlined here below.

These are the tricks of the trade. If topiary is only a little over 2m high then standing on a box or stepping stool, as found in most homes for reaching top shelves and cleaning internal windows, can be used.

Weeding box edging prior to clipping.

Over time the topiary has been partially shaped by the access available. As well as space and time, access will always limit the possible shape.

A box either side of a flower bed with a plank laid across the space between enables access to the bed and to topiary in its centre without trampling on the plants.

The next line of attack would be to use trestles supporting planks. This will also span plantings. Care needs to be taken to place blocks under the feet of the trestles to prevent them from sinking into soft earth and also to ensure that they are vertical and the planks on top level. These are often used to give a platform at a height of about 2m (6.5ft).

For work above 4m (13ft) lightweight scaffolding is used, or in some cases mobile hydraulic work platforms. These provide a very safe and stable

Using a scaffolding platform to reach the giant specimens at Levens Hall.

The pinnacle of topiary maintenance at Levens. However safe the scaffolding platform is, you still need a head for heights. This illustrates why a regime of once a year clipping is maintained in historic topiary gardens.

operating area to virtually any height when used by professionals according to the manufacturer's guidelines.

The scaffolding system, in particular, has the advantage that it can be erected just about anywhere and to practically any height, and certainly to any height required in a garden, without resorting to tree climbing. The only disadvantage is that rising vertically from the ground it does not permit access to narrow and pointed topiary tops.

Hydraulic work platforms do not suffer from this problem, since they are able to reach out to some extent. They do, however, need stable, firm ground access and cannot always fit into the garden area.

CHAPTER 7

Hedges

DESIGN PRINCIPLES

Although the topiary purist may suggest that hedges should not be covered in a book such as this, in reality the dividing line between hedges and topiary is often blurred. Topiary shapes of one kind or another are often to be seen sprouting from hedging and, likewise, decorative hedges with scalloped tops and features bursting from their sides cannot be regarded as other than topiary. Unadorned hedges are often closely linked with topiary gardens.

Hedges of all sorts are basically used to define space within a large garden, act as a barrier defining property in smaller gardens, and, as lower hedges, act as borders and form patterns in parterres and knot gardens. As visual barriers to wall in garden spaces hedges rarely need to be higher than 2m (6.5ft) and just dense enough in character to prevent a view through (15cm/6in wide may well be enough). There is no extra benefit to be gained from losing garden space to wider hedging.

As physical barriers, hedges can be created dense enough to repel humans and livestock, and prickly plants are an obvious choice for this purpose.

While hedges can be low enough to step over they still act as barriers, psychologically conditioning responses to the garden space. They can direct movement as well as contain planting and are growing expressions of the divisions that form the layout of the garden. They may be used to frame vistas and act as a thematic link throughout the garden. In a topiary garden they provide thematic continuity without over-use of decorative shapes.

Hedges can of course be strictly geometrical in shape and profile and this is probably the first impression that comes to mind when you think of a hedge. Hedge plantings, however, can be used in

The satisfying line of a freshly clipped hedge.

Access space between border and hedge.

a looser, more informal manner, with the individual plants that constitute the hedge allowed to grow out informally. They thus express more of their nature as plants and can be shaped into what is known as cloud hedging. A mixed species hedge might invite this development.

The Importance of Access

Whichever type of hedge is used and whatever its size, it is important that the area of access is given suitable thought and consideration. Access will, of course, be needed for clipping, and it must be remembered that the hedge will be considerably wider before its clipping than afterwards and also will increase in width slightly year by year as it grows. This should be borne in mind from the start and due allowance for incremental growth incorporated at the design and planting stage. Space around the hedge is also needed for the good of the hedge itself. If planting is carried on right up to the hedge, then lack of light here during the growing season will weaken and eventually kill its lower branches. Where hedges stand behind borders it is far better that a clear pathway is left between the hedge and the border. This is better for the border and is far better for the health and maintenance of the hedge. Where hedges are used on a large scale, access should also be provided for wheeled trestles, scaffolding or the mobile work platform which will be needed for maintenance clipping. Even a box to stand on requires firm, level space. Matters of access need to be considered at the design stage.

Hedge Layout

When planning a garden layout, design or development, it is useful to incorporate any desired hedging from the start. Like walls and fences, they function as part of the architectural infrastructure of the garden. Typical situations involving hedges include boundaries between properties, divisions between areas within the garden and the delineation and emphasis of features such as pathways and vistas, as well as enclosing flower borders. Large-scale planning on paper or computer may be used to record and communicate design decisions, but the real planning takes place in the mind and on the ground.

Once more absorbing the genius of the place and the character of the garden over time can facilitate decision making. A few notes or a sketch on the back of an envelope or drawn on a photograph can help to achieve good design decisions appropriate for the garden in question. Imposing set ideas on paper may create a design but not necessarily a personal garden filled with confident and subjective preferences.

Once the scheme is decided upon, the idea must be transferred to the ground. Sticks, canes, string lines, hosepipes, marker paint sprays or dry sand are all part of the tools used in marking out a hedge. Although an exact replica of a plan can be made on the ground – scaled up by using tape measures and marker canes – this should be seen only as the first stage of transferring a plan to reality.

Gardens are partly natural in that they are seldom confined to precise geometrical accordances with buildings and straight lines, and away from the drawing board a garden's irregularities become noticeable. It is best to live with the marked-out design for some time before transferring it into living hedging material. All the dimensions and implications of the design need to sink into the consciousness before actual ground work begins. This is not time wasted but rather intelligent anticipation that may preclude the need for any future problem solving.

HEDGE PLANTING

Site preparation is essentially similar to that for individual topiary planting and indeed for any shrub – the difference will be the scale of the operation and its linear nature. As in all planting, time and trouble expended at the onset will repay generously over the years, particularly in those early years when there is an eagerness to see rapid growth to the desired stature as soon as possible.

Thorough working of the soil, incorporating organic material, will be greatly appreciated by the young plants. Individual planting pockets are not practical, so a wide strip along the projected hedge line should be cultivated. It should be about three times the width of the individual plants. Deeper digging is often recommended but in reality 30cm (12in) or so will be sufficient as roots more naturally spread outwards than downwards.

Beyond soil structure and fertility, the main consideration to be addressed is of course drainage. This is particularly important where yew is to be used, as this much-used and favoured hedging subject is particularly prone to waterborne disease. Where the land is generally well drained there should be no problems. Borderline areas where land is sticky and wet, even if only occasionally after heavy rainfall, require more attention to drainage from the start. The planting trench itself should become a drainage channel as its more open and disturbed soil will gather and hold water from surrounding areas.

One solution is to lay a drainage line along the length of the new hedging and continue it beyond into a soakaway. Alternatively, plant the hedge on a low mound of soil, thus providing a low, relatively drier substrate for initial establishment.

CHOICE OF PLANT MATERIAL

There are several factors governing the choice of species to plant. Firstly the projected ultimate size needs to be considered: box can be clipped low as an edging plant whereas yew will grow quickly to 2m (6.5ft) or more. Then the desired effect will depend on the choice of evergreen or deciduous material, small-leaved or large-leaved, foliage colour and variegation, and the presence of noticeable flowers and berries. How fast the plant grows is also a consideration with regard to maintenance, while hardiness, climatic requirements and wind and salt resistance are other considerations.

Hedging plants are obviously all planted at approximately the same size, but the starting size can vary enormously; the larger the plants the higher the initial financial outlay. Although instant effect is much prized in contemporary gardening, a hedge is a long-term investment, and it must be emphasized that smaller plants establish themselves faster and will catch up with and eventually overtake identical species planted at a larger size. Unless an instant effect is needed, settle for patiently watching the growth of smaller plants.

Containerized plants can, in theory, be planted all year round, but if planted in late spring or early summer they will need to be kept well watered during dry spells. After a year or so the roots should have escaped from the planting trench and spread into the surrounding soil so additional watering should not be necessary. When planting containerized plants always ensure that the plants have not become pot-bound, or else the encircling roots, confined by the period spent in the pot, will in time strangle the trunk. If this seems to be a problem, tease the roots out before planting.

Bare-root or root-balled plants should only be planted during their dormant season; they often prove as satisfactory as containerized stock at a fraction of the price. Once again, watering during the first season may prove necessary. Whichever type of stock is planted, it should never be planted deeper than the depth to which it has been growing, and the individual plants should be well firmed in without compacting the soil.

INITIAL FORMATIVE PRUNING

During the first season following their planting many hedging plants will make little or no growth. This is a perfectly natural reaction to the move and although there is little top growth, there will be plenty of new root activity as they become established in their new environment. It is therefore wise not to cut the bushes back in any way during their first year unless root loss has been very severe at planting, in which case some top growth may be removed after planting in order balance up the plants.

From the second season onwards, clipping should be performed at least annually to help make the hedge dense and uniform. Often during the early years of establishing a hedge some plants will grow more vigorously than others and trimming them back to a level top line will help achieve the uniformity required.

The ideal profile for a hedge would be wide at the bottom with sloping sides or a batter to a narrower top. This allows for more light to reach the base and thereby thicken the growth there. Until the required height is reached the top should only be cut back lightly each year – that is to say, enough to keep the hedge even and encourage vigorous side growth below.

Old mobile platform that just fits the space between hedge and fence.

HEDGE TRIMMING

In theory the ideal cross-section of a hedge would present a strong, central leader supporting a thick mass of horizontal branches furnishing the outer walls. Strong upright growths on the outside of the hedge are detrimental to the shape of the hedge, as they tend to take over and then sag outwards. It is best to remove them as they occur.

Very low hedges, for example the low box hedges used in parterres, are back-breaking to clip. Here, very long strimmers supported from a standing position make for better posture. Otherwise kneeling using protective knee-pads may help. Long, high hedges may be accessed easily from wheel staging, scaffold towers or self-propelled hydraulic lifts. It all depends on the size and scale of the hedge.

When clipping a hedge it is always advisable to make the first cuts in the thickest growth areas, which will be cut back hardest to give the final line. Weaker areas can then be trimmed back less severely to even matters up. Cutting the weaker growth first tends to result in cutting too far, making it difficult to match up the thicker areas.

String lines used as guides for perfectly level cutting can be troublesome, either catching on twigs

Cutting low box edging with electric clippers.

or getting cut by the clippers. Laser levels may at some stage be developed into useful tools for hedge clippers and topiarists, but at present the best way of eradicating discrepancies is still simply to eye up the hedge along its length. A taut string line placed vertically along a hedge, or indeed a cane, can be a useful point of reference without interfering in the clipping.

If you notice minor discrepancies along the hedge after clipping but are unable to deal with them immediately, take notes that you can refer to the following season.

DECORATIVE HEDGES

If you are aiming for a crenellated hedge or one with decorative features growing out of the top, it is best to plan for this from the very start. Finials, peacocks and any topiary work extending above the hedge top line are better supported if a main trunk lies directly beneath them.

CHAPTER 8

Simple Shapes

Pruning trees and shrubs to emphasize their natural form is the province of bonsai or perhaps tree surgery at its very best, for example when managing specimen trees in parks and gardens, botanical collections or arboreta. Topiary is the creative opposite: training and maintaining wonderful, contrived, artificial and unnatural shapes. It is living, green sculpture, and as an art form has thread its course through the long history of the garden.

Any interest in topiary is in a long-term, ongoing process. There are no perfect, instant results, although the revival of interest in topiary means that ready-made specimens can be bought at a price, and frames and shapes in chicken wire or wire outlines can be bought as guidelines. For the topiarist it is the changing shape as a specimen grows over time that is the challenge. There are no completed end points to arrive at, as topiary is either maintained carefully and regularly or it grows out of its creative form and reverts to a state of nature. Clipping should be carried out as described in Chapter 6, even if the final shape has not been achieved, in order to encourage dense growth and the bushy, close surface desired.

BALLS

These are the most basic and easy shape to produce initially and are often seen cut from box. Untrimmed and untrained specimens are often naturally simply a rough spherical shape, and easy trimming will tighten up this form. They also look good in pots.

It is possible just to trim the bush all over (standing back often to view progress) with shears to achieve this shape. For greater precision a series of circular bands can be cut round the plant and then joined up to form the spherical shape desired.

Almost afloat on grass at Wollerton Old Hall, Shropshire, these classic box hemispheres are anchored by the weight of their form.

At Wollerton Old Hall this evocation of an Edwardian garden uses the repetition and reflection of box hemispheres in a formal manner to create a mood of calm and contemplation.

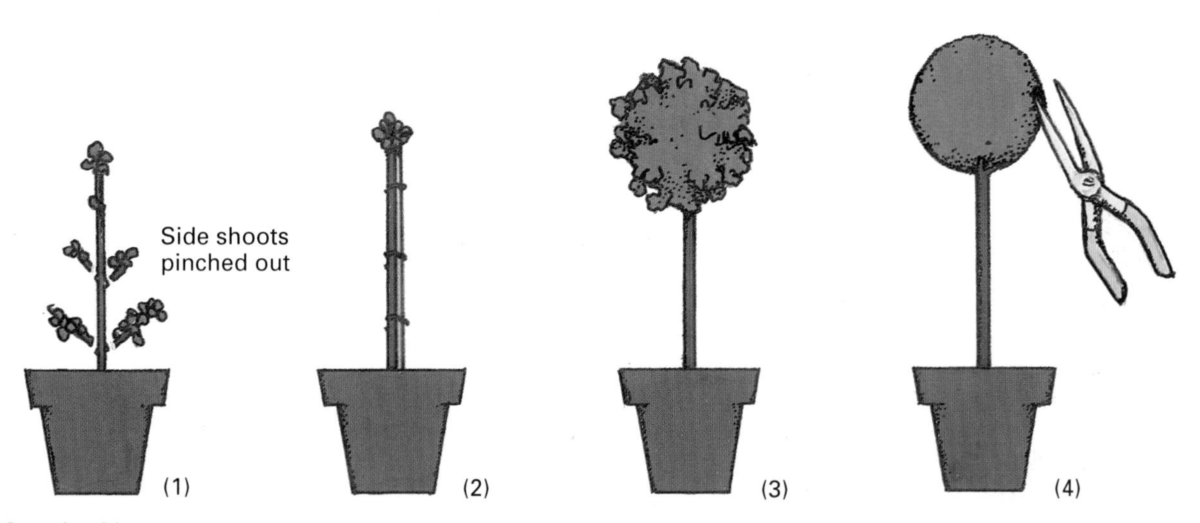

Standard box

Standards are part of display gardening and floristry covering every possible plant from cacti to fuchsias, roses and lavender. Box is a perfect topiary plant for this treatment, and a pair of box standards can be grown quite quickly.

1. Plant a box plant – even a rooted cutting works well here – in the centre of a pot. Pinch out side rigorously until a single central stem is growing. Insert a cane to support this leader shoot, and take care not to damage it.

2. When the plant has reached the desired height, mark it on the vertical cane, clean the stem of all growth and pinch out the top shoots.

3. This encourages thicker growth at the top.

4. Shape the ball at the top of the stem with hand shears or secateurs.

Although initially easy to form, balls do prove harder to maintain over time as the overhung growth at the bottom tends to grow very little and ultimately loses its leaves. Atop there will be a tendency towards verticality and the upward growth may result in an elongated egg shape. This could provide alternative forms to adapt the plant into. A more sustainable shape is the hemisphere, which conforms to the principle of wider growth at the base narrowing at the top. Both these shapes can be developed in time by allowing the strongest central leader to grow on upwards and stacked shapes to be created.

CONES

The cone is one of the basic topiary shapes and certainly one of the most important. Many plants grow naturally into an approximation of a cone shape. They can be seen in many differing sizes either as solitary specimens or punctuation marks along low box hedging. Ideally a plant with a single, vertical leader should be chosen and any competitors removed. While strictly speaking the single leader is not essential, the basic cone shape is often grown on into other, more complex, vertical forms

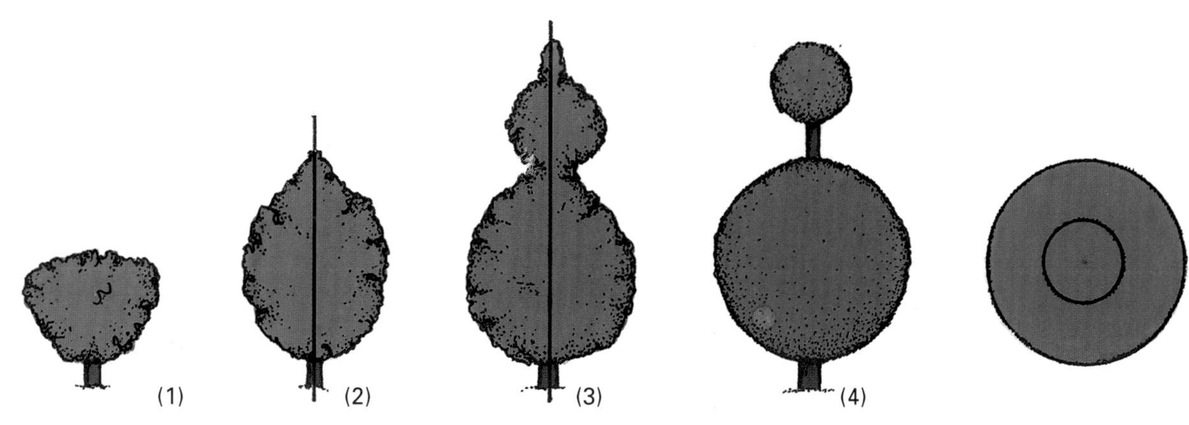

Sphere on sphere in box

1. Plant the box (in or out of a container) and allow it to grow into a sphere.
2. Encourage a central leader shoot to grow vertically from the centre of the sphere, possibly marked temporarily by cane so you can check it is truly vertical with a level.
3. When the upper growth reaches the same sort of size as the lower sphere its clipping can begin.
4. The result is a very pleasing representation of balance and equilibrium. Box spheres alone can look as if they are liable to roll around a garden, whereas one balancing another appears more static.

Using string as a guideline for scribing a circular drum at the base of specimen topiary.

and a sturdy, strong central leader would be beneficial to this enhancement of the basic shape.

Cones can also be cut into pyramids, and whether square or circular at the base a long, straight edge – a cane or pole – is very handy when clipping them to help define a true face or angle. Although a cone is circular in plan it is often better to cut a number of perfectly flat facets on the sides of the shape first of all, making it in effect a pyramid. These can then be chamfered and merged into one another to create the perfect cone with circular cross-sections. It is best to start on the shoulders of the shapes where the growth is thickest, and work up and down to a predetermined straight edge. Lighter clipping above and below the shoulders will maintain the line from top to bottom.

Age-old spiral in the foreground at Levens.

A box spiral that over time has grown into a shell-like form. Age softens the strictest of shapes.

Snow on a spiral shell at Levens.

Cones are inherently good shapes for the plant, being wider at the bottom and tapering towards the top. This ensures good light reaches all surfaces. They can be maintained well almost indefinitely and often only suffer when clipped so tightly that growth and development are inhibited. Cones benefit from being allowed to grow slightly larger each year.

As you become more confident you can even use the cone as the launching point for some more

A line of cones as an exercise in repeated, overlapping forms working beautifully.

String used as guideline for cutting a spiral into a cone.

ornamental development; for example, you could cut a spiral into it, slice tiers out of them, or perhaps develop a finial decoration from the leader shoot. In containers, cones make symmetrical pairs (which benefit from rotation if close to buildings or walls), although yew is perhaps too vigorous for this application.

CUBES

In the topiary repertoire cubes are quite literally the building blocks of squared-off planes. This shape could be extended upwards into a Stonehenge-type monolith and add variety to a hedge in yew. Initially a light squaring-off of the untrimmed bush will start the progress towards densely surfaced planes. Trimming back the top will of course encourage the sides to fill out well.

Topiary cones along a caravan side.

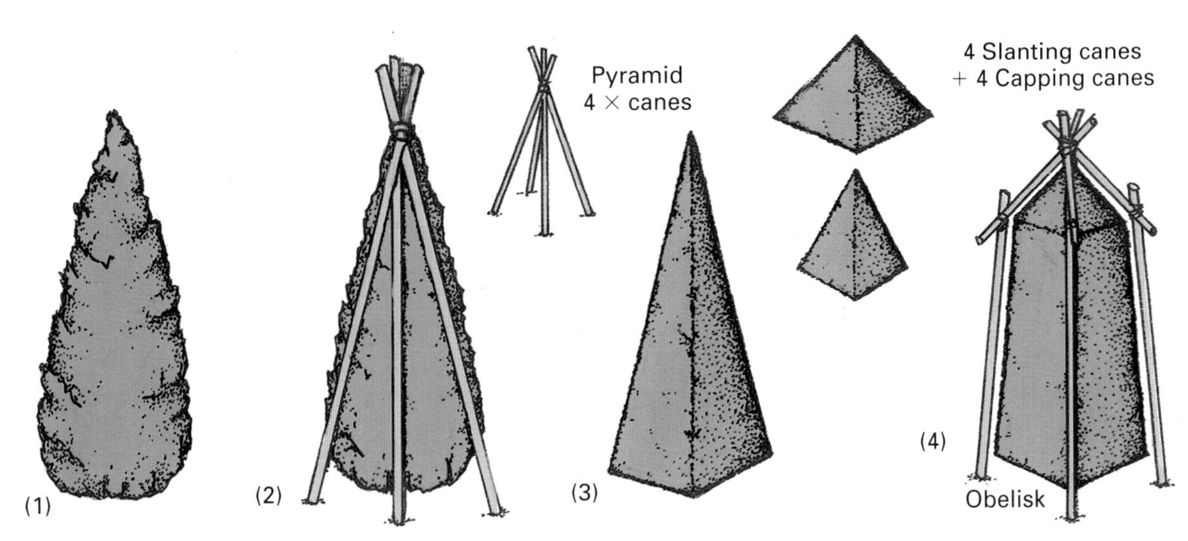

Obelisk or pyramid in yew
1. Yew is the most architectural of topiary plants and an obelisk or pyramid is a strikingly monumental geometric form. A pair of them may flank a path where it leads onto a lawn or terminate a vista in a long garden. The initial work requires the growth of a yew plant with a strong central leader stem to approximately the required height. Because it is a geometric operation you will need straight canes when the shaping begins.
2. For a pyramid, space four canes of suitable length evenly around the topiary yew at the desired angle. This will involve marking out their position on the ground close to the plant and the best way to measure their distance is by attaching a loop of garden twine or string to the central trunk of the plant. For geometrical precision the canes need to be equidistant and then joined with wire or twine at the top.
3. When the yew has clearly grown beyond the imaginary surface plane between the canes, trim it back with shears or electric clippers (shears are safer if canes are being used). Eventually, over several years, the surface growth of the yew will thicken up and the canes will need to be removed in order to cut the angles to a sharp point.
Pyramids look good when a group of several are placed together, particularly when they vary in size and height.
4. For an obelisk the four corner canes do not meet at the top and their angle is much steeper, in fact almost vertical. Once the growth of the yew has arrived at approximately the desired height, mark out a miniature pyramid with four small canes at the top of the obelisk column. This creates the apex of the obelisk.
Where space and resources permit, obelisks and pyramids look extremely effective aligned along the length of a garden. If they diminish in height, this gives the illusion of greater depth. Likewise, a single feature obelisk at the end of a vista in a garden can suggest greater space and depth in the garden by being smaller than expected. People expect the height to be around 2m (6.5ft), about the same as a largish person.

Formal parterre with topiary cones as vertical punctuation marks.

Cleaning the stem of a spiral shape that is just within reach of a standing gardener.

New growth glows on a yew spiral.

The top surface is best eyed on the level by getting a view directly across it, and if possible assessing against a horizontal line, such as a roof line or a wall top. You can check how the verticals relate to the top visually with string and weight plumblines.

Cubes are a very durable shape. They will last and expand readily so long as they are kept free from competition and are well lit. The main problem to avoid is the bases at the sides becoming overhung and thus thinning out. Ultimately, the cube may lose some definition as it grows more on its sunny side, but this can be remedied by a compensating lighter cut on the northern side. There may come a time when the shapes begin to look squashy and lose some of their geometric precision. This characterful variation may prove desirable as they bulge and lean away from the perpendicular.

CYLINDERS

Cylinders as a shape may prove as challenging as any of the other geometric shapes because they have such a precise and perfect shape, with their straight sides and circular, drum-like plan. Any deviation from perfection is blatant and immediately picked up on by the viewer.

They are not unusually difficult but like any upright and vertical-sided topiary shape the lower areas, particularly on the northern side, are likely to be sparse and weak-growing. This needs to be watched for when clipping and extra growth left there if needed to compensate.

Remember the principle that, whatever the shape, it is always best to begin clipping at the highest and thickest growth. Cut back to the determining line here, then match all other areas up with it. It is all too easy to round off the tops of the verticals too, losing their crispness and creating a sausage shape. These shoulders are going to be the most vigorous growing area. Again beware of this and step back to view your work frequently. Using a plumbline can inspire confidence and confirm the eyeing-in.

Cylinders are a relatively sustainable shape over time, particularly when attention is given to the verticality of the sides and ultimately to their circular cross-section. In order to avoid their becoming oval shaped a circular mat of lightweight material could be placed on the top. Most topiary shapes are defined by the eye and in many cases geometric precision is not absolutely necessary to give an interesting shape.

SPIRALS

Of the simple shapes these are the most impressive and complex to attain. They can sometimes be cut out of existing cones or developed from much younger specimens, or youngish specimens already trained could be bought in to provide a model for further specimens. Of all the shapes these require the straightest, most dominant leader stem as it is from this that all the other branches radiate, and their unifying mass of foliage creates the spiral. Basic formation involves cutting a slot back through the foliage to the main trunk then extending this upwards going round the piece. In theory a unified slot should be formed leaving a raised spiral of growth around the trunk. You can wind a string line around the plant initially to help visualize the shape and if necessary regulate and adjust the line of cut. You can leave it on as a guideline, but like all string lines, it can end up just getting in the way. Once you have decided on the line it is probably best to cut freehand.

You will see that if any strong vertical growths are cut away to form one part of the spiral, their upper parts will also come out, removing higher parts of the topiary. This is why the key feature of a plant chosen for creating a spiral needs to be horizontal radiating growth coming from the central leader. Spirals are most easily created from tall, thin shapes, whose lower areas are allowed to grow out horizontally later once the basic shape has been formed.

Shaping a spiral may seem to be reducing an alarming quantity of plant material and may look a sorry sight to begin with. This is not a moment for panic, as time is needed for gaps to fill in and the irregularities to smooth over and the shape become denser. After a few cycles of growth and clipping the definitive spiral will be formed, and you will see where to clip to enhance the distinctive shape. The finished beauty is well worth the effort and the waiting.

Spirals are also a sustainable shape in that once formed the lower tiers may be allowed to grow out, forming a much better shape and lessening the stark verticality of its formative phases. This follows

A Dutch garden showing a potted yew spiral.

The finished spiral. It has a long way to grow but the shape has been determined and no one working on this specimen in the future would attempt to impose another shape upon it.

Spiral specimens in pots along the wall of a garden. This Dutch garden is a telling reminder that a shape such as a spiral really needs a strong base out of which to rise to be effective, and none works better than a container.

the principle of wider at the bottom, narrower at the top. With denser growth the top of one spiral may merge with the next turn above it. This can be avoided by more severe clipping to emphasize the slots and spaces between the twists of the spiral. Missed shoots must also be prevented from forming vertical growth, which will confuse the outline of the shape. If the chosen specimen is not strongly vertical through a single leader stem, then a spiral shape incised into it could produce a tram-line spiral effect, which may be difficult to maintain and if cut too deeply may cause layers to flop under their own weight. A spiral shape can also be allowed to blur and soften into a shape more like a snail shell. Like all art forms, a topiary spiral is a point of departure and there is room and invitation to improvise.

Contrast between clean stem and foliage in a 'form on form' specimen.

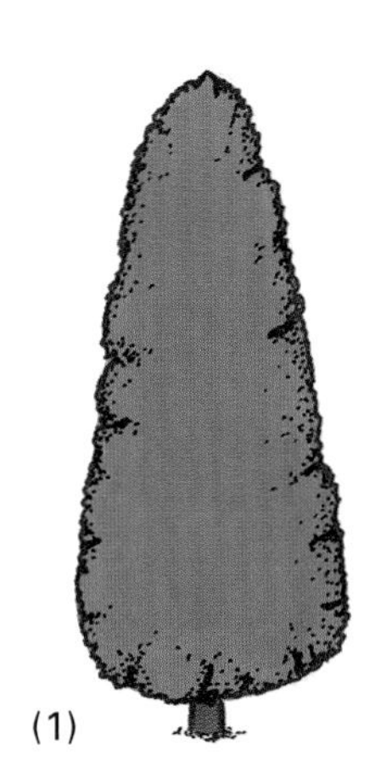
(1)

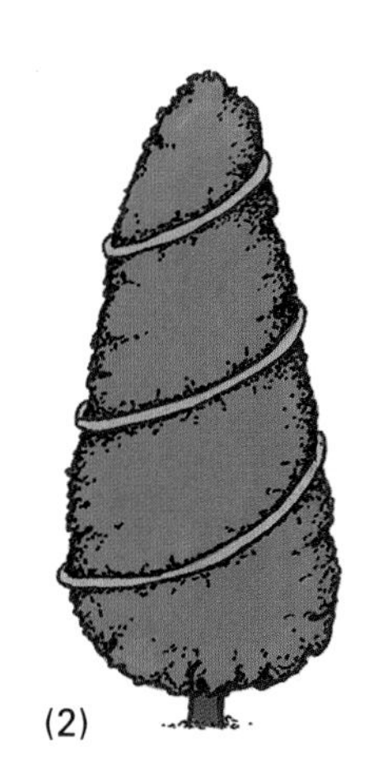
(2)

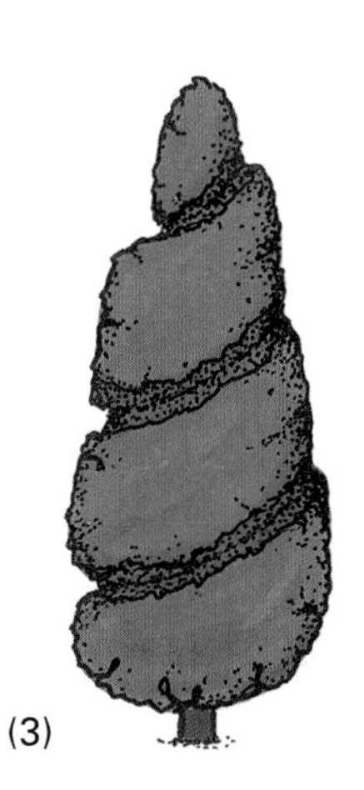
(3)

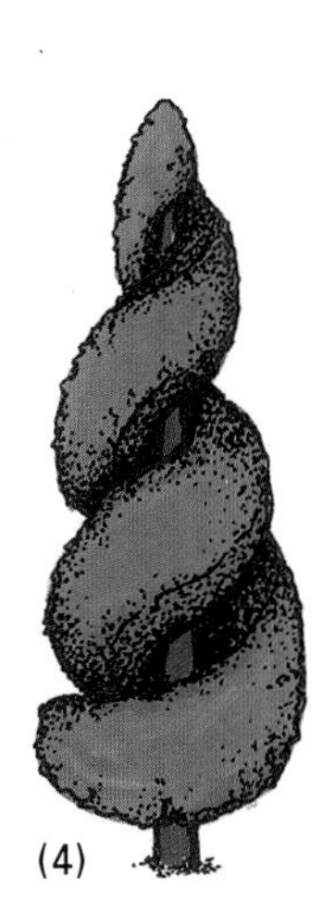
(4)

A simple spiral in box or yew

1. The starting point of a spiral is a basic cone. This should have a single, central leader trunk. Grow it to the required height or plant as a pre-grown shrub and allow it to settle in and put out new root growth before training begins. Initial training should take place in spring when the shrub is beginning its new growth.

2. Before delineating the spiral on the surface of the topiary cone it needs to be clipped smooth, removing the new growth back to that of the previous year. Wind garden twine or string around the specimen, leaving about 30cm (12in) space between the lines.

3. Using secateurs, cut a 'bite' into the flat surface of the topiary, following the line from the base to the tip. While moving around the specimen, remove more growth successively until the trunk at the centre of the specimen is gradually exposed.

4. This process of removal will eventually reveal the spiral shape. Initially the space between each coil of the spiral needs to be exaggerated in order to permit light to enter and new growth to take place.

The result of the first season's clipping may look a little sparse to start with, but once the new growth appears you will soon realize how important it is to maintain an annual regime of cleaning up the spiral form. Although this is a relatively simple shape it depends on the clear definition of its form for success and if neglected would soon grow back into a cone again.

CHAPTER 9

Complex and Figurative Shapes

This is where imagination and inspiration can come out to play. As long as you respect your topiary as living plant material and not treat it like modelling clay and bear in mind the principle of plant growth being wider at the bottom and tapering as it rises, the rest is up to you. The variety of topiary forms and shapes is really quite vast.

Inspiration can be derived from many published sources and from visits to gardens open to the public. Garden centres and specialist nurseries can supply wire frameworks and chicken-wire shapes to act as aids to creative topiary. Clipping can run to abstract or freehand shapes and new topiary, as it is called, is the latest phase in the long history of this ancient art of clipping. In its most uninhibited form new topiary can be said to liberate the art from its historical associations and allow creativity free rein. It is very much practised in the USA and derives many ideas from the Far East. It also looks back across two millennia to the *ars topiaria* of classical Rome and in itself is a revival of the expressiveness of topiary at the height of its sophistication; by sophistication here we mean the boldness and assertiveness of fashion statements before they are absorbed into the mainstream of the art they express.

As topiary shapes become more complex, so the need for some underlying support framework of wood, metal or wire becomes more pressing. Ideally, these should be temporary wherever possible, but a lot of chicken-wire shapes and in particular wire frameworks for ivy to grow over would be impossible to remove and simply become hidden by the plant material in time. Wire ties and supports can in time do untold damage to the plant material and can strangle and slice stems as they grow through the constrictions designed to shape them. This is where string has an advantage, as it rots and can be replaced when necessary. A balance has to be maintained between gardening for posterity and for almost immediate gratification. It is respect for plant material and the principles of good management which have permitted historic topiary gardens to thrive and survive.

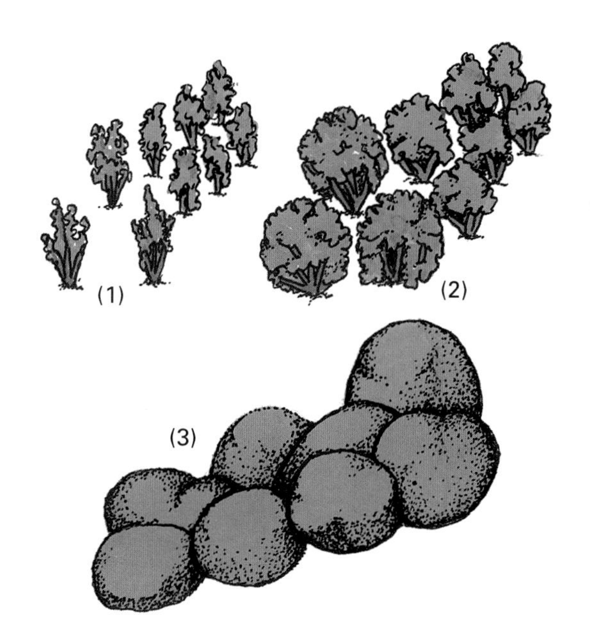

Abstract lonicera landscape/land art

Lonicera grows very quickly and demands a lot of clipping so is an excellent subject for freehand topiary work. It thrives in the shade and can be planted as a row of merging forms to create a landscape hedge – a piece of land art, in fact.
1. These plants are cheap and are easily raised from cuttings. However many are needed, plant them approx 1m (3ft) apart and staggered informally.
2. As the growth of the plants increases cut off the tips of shoots constantly to encourage the plants to thicken up.
3. Constant clipping in an informal manner will create boulder-like green shapes that will eventually merge. Where they merge it is important to clip closely with secateurs to maintain the distinctness of the forms.

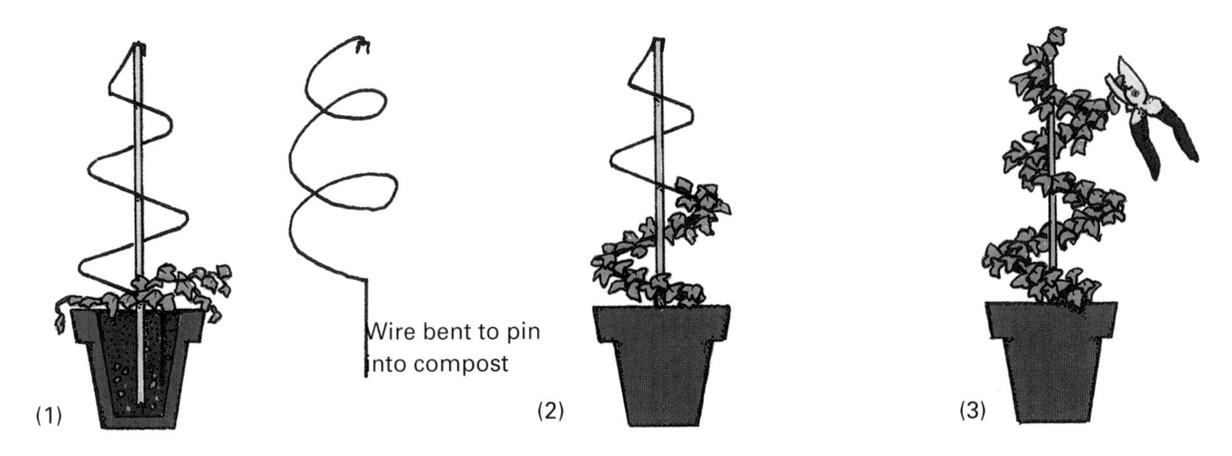

Making an ivy spiral
This is an effective and decorative idea to create in a pot. Ivy spirals look good inside marquees at weddings with lights attached, they make very pleasing gifts and, at a smaller size, make conversation pieces as table decorations. Wire spirals can be bought ready prepared but since wire is invariably sold in coils it is effectively ready to use as purchased.
1. Place a hollow bamboo cane to the desired height (at least twice the height of the pot) in the centre of a pot filled with heavy compost (with added grit). Bend one end of a length of coiled wire into a straight length to pin it into the compost. The first coil of the spiral should be the circumference of the pot and the coils then get progressively smaller until you reach the top of the cane. Fasten the wire by bending it into the top of the hollow cane.
2. Plant three long, rooted shoots at the base of the wire, and wrap them around the wire as they grow.
3. Feed the ivy well with liquid fertilizer for speedy growth. If necessary, tie the ivy to the wire with garden twine or raffia. Occasional groomings with secateurs will maintain the spiral shape.
It is always a good idea to make at least a pair of these at a time. One is never enough.

Topiary is an art form and should be enjoyed for itself and the pleasure it affords the creator and the spectator. While figurative shapes almost break the rule that topiary is not an end-product in itself but continues to grow, they are very much a challenge to stylization. Topiary animals raise many cheerful smiles because they do not represent closely the model they are following. The delight perhaps lies in the fact that such approximations to animal forms are at all possible using plant material.

TIERED COMBINATION SHAPES

These are basically shape upon shape with bare trunk separating the layers, for example a series of balls decreasing in size, or a cake-stand, or fountain. They could be a cube base with a sphere on top then a finial rising above. They are in fact combinations of the simple shapes described in the previous chapter and may be developed from the creation of a successful base shape extended upwards through letting the leader stem grow on vertically. This is a slow process of additive topiary, year on year, but has the advantage of not requiring the topiarist to create a tall, complex structure from the start. In attempting work of this kind the choice of shoot for the new leader is very important. Not only must it be centrally positioned in relation to the existing and projected shapes, but it has also to lead from a lower leader shoot in order to give maximum support to what develops above. This will project the weight of each additional tier vertically down to the earth for optimum stability.

It is well worth looking carefully into the existing tier for the right shoot with which to continue upwards. Even if it looks thin and puny it will strengthen up with time and develop appropriate proportions in relation to the thickness of growth it sustains.

Tiered forms may also be cut out of larger existing shapes. Large cones are the most amenable to this treatment. If care has been taken in encouraging a strong central leader, with horizontal, radiating growth and no competitive leaders, then this

Training giraffes out of lonicera using wire.

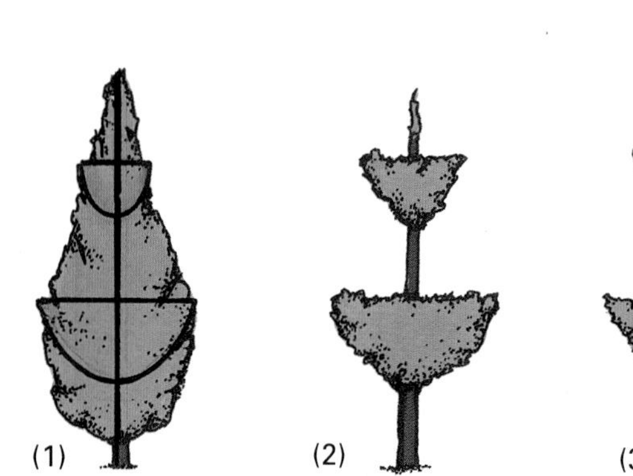
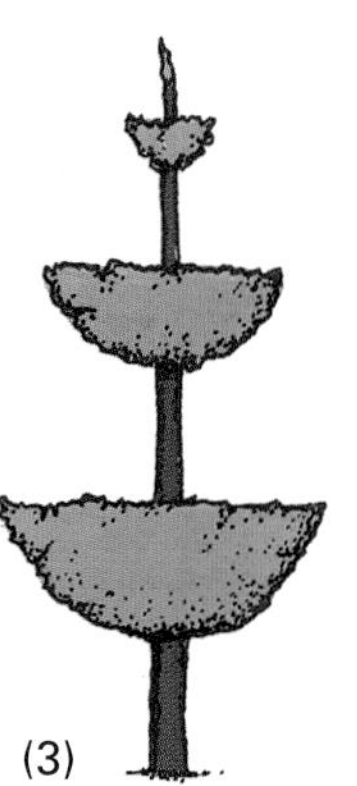
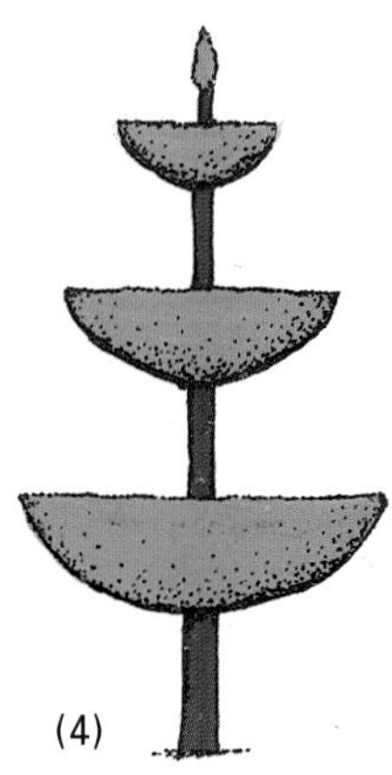

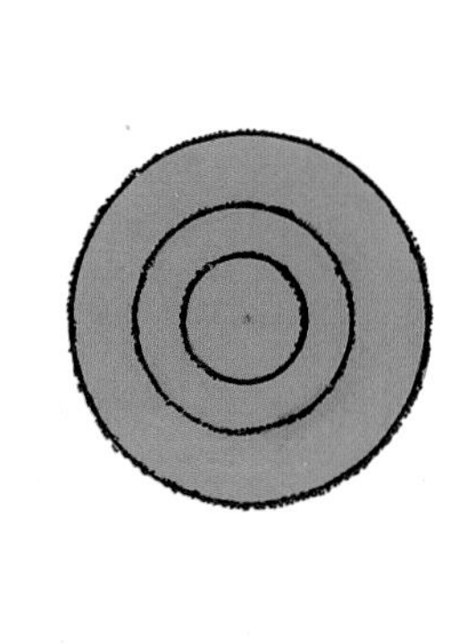

Shape on shape: tiered cake-stand or fountain in yew
This is a classic historic form found in medieval manuscripts and seen in historic gardens. It is possible to buy these already prepared, which is advisable as the alternative is to wait for a yew to grow to about 2m (6.5ft) or to buy in an unprepared shrub of that height, which may lack the essential central, vertical stem.
1. However you decide to do it, you will need an established, strongly growing yew 2m (6.5ft) high with a vertical and straight leader trunk at the centre.
2. Separate the foliage growth into layers or stages with clear stem dividing them. Start 1.5m (5ft) from the ground to give a sturdy, clear base to the first tier of the specimen. The second stage can be half this distance above and the third slightly less.
3. Training involves keeping the clear stem clean of adventitious, regenerative yew shoots and every spring also clipping the growth of the stages with secateurs. The emphasis is on allowing the horizontal shoots to grow outwards.
4. Once the tier has reached the desired size, trim the rim with secateurs. To ensure symmetry, attach a loop of string to the trunk and move it around the tier to act as a guide to a flat surface and a constant radial depth.

will be ideal. Peering into the shape to study its supporting branch structures carefully before choosing the exact placement of the tiers is time well spent. When all is decided cut boldly back to the main trunk between each desired tier. After a few years of growth and careful clipping the shapes will tighten up considerably.

In time, problems may arise with symmetrical specimens with remarkable silhouettes under constant admiration and inspection. In a tiered cake-stand or series of discs it is often the case that the tiers incline towards an oval shape towards the faster growing side. This clearly distorts the symmetry and outline of the shape. A loop of string

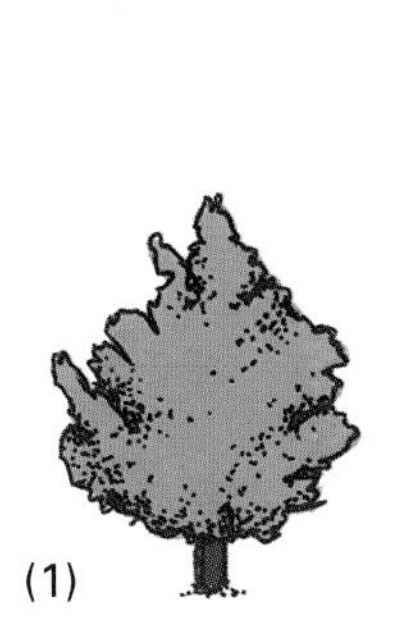

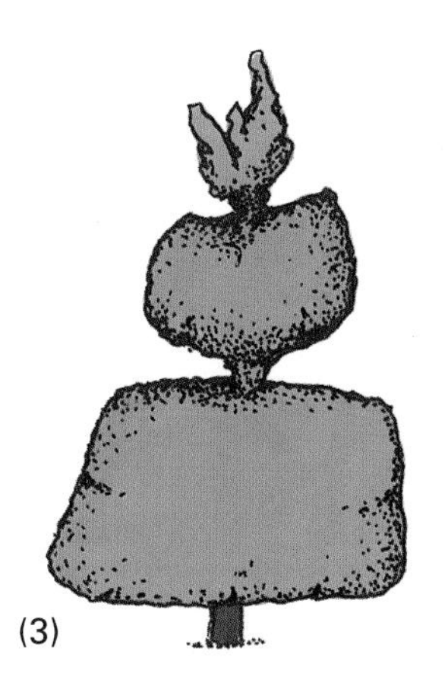

Informal shape on shape
Organic/amorphous yew
Yew provides probably the best sculptural topiary work as it is dense, solid and weighty, making it look as substantial and permanent as it is.
To grow an amorphous or organic topiary specimen is to be open to every form of inspiration and to work freehand in topiary is a truly relaxing and therapeutic creative art. If there is a yew tree in the garden already this is one way of making it into a point of interest visually and sculpturally.
1. Allow the planted yew to establish and keep it lightly clipped at the sides all round to concentrate the new growth. It is attractive to keep the trunk clean near the ground to suggest that the sculptural work is elevated and also to clip the bottom edge sharply.
2. Top growth is concentrated into a leader, which may be eccentric and allowed to grow out to one side. Make sure it is separated from the lower mass by clean stem.
3. Encourage a finial to develop out of the second layer. This, again, rises from clean stem.
4. When the topmost section has grown to the desired size you can tighten up the clipping. The surfaces do not need to be flat as long as they tend to be wider at the base and light is allowed to reach all surface areas. The finished result is a tottering feature reminiscent of prehistory or a Dartmoor tor, but above all sculptural and entirely unique.

around the trunk set to a desired length will act as a set of compasses when rotated so that the circular tiers can be reset. It is also possible that in time the top of one tier may grow up to join the bottom the next one up. This is best avoided by cutting large spaces initially or removing the bottoms of tiers by clipping. In severe cases you can take drastic action and remove alternate tiers.

Where topiary specimen pieces are created or developed, shape upon shape, with no clear area of trunk dividing sections, there is always the danger of shoots from one shape growing up and invading part of the superior section. In time these areas become more apparent as they are less well supported than the tier they have penetrated and tend to flop about. Removal will lead unavoidably to gaps being created, so this problem is best tackled as early as possible.

ARCHITECTURAL FORMS

While topiary is generally considered to be green, living sculpture it can have architectural significance. To link architecture and sculpture many details from buildings can be created as topiary pieces, including finials, window arches, chimney features and obelisks. Archways and bridges can be created, as well as bowers and even hiding places for children to play in or garden furniture to be stored. Of course, hedges are intrinsically green walls and therefore architectural.

The general principles of topiary still apply; afford full light to all surfaces and ensure that surfaces intended to be vertical or horizontal are true. Wooden or metal frameworks may be needed in the early stages here and again it is best to use string ties which rot easily to avoid damaging the plant.

Topiary reflecting the form of the buildings it stands next to.

Pierced hedging as architecture, topiary and an invitation to pass beyond.

Once growth has taken off and hardened into position the supports can be removed. It is often better to leave it undisturbed rather than risk damage to the green structure.

CRENELLATIONS

A special mention should be made of these castellated features, which are usually cut into hedge. Like all superstructured topiary features they need to rise from strong supporting growth below. They will lose definition over time but add interest to hedgetops. Where a hedge is a boundary and conceals either part of the garden or the view beyond, thought may be given to creating a window in the hedge. This needs to be considered in the early stages as the hedge will need to be grown around the window space.

LETTERS AND NUMBERS

Another return to classical Rome is the laying out of box hedges in the form of letters to create names, which ideally need to be viewed from above. Even a pair of entwined initials would make a suitable commemoration of a family event.

Letters can, of course, also be created vertically with their difficulty depending on the letter required. The principles are the same as for training any topiary growth. The letter A could be formed from two bushes (fastigiate yews for example) trained upwards to meet and form a pointed

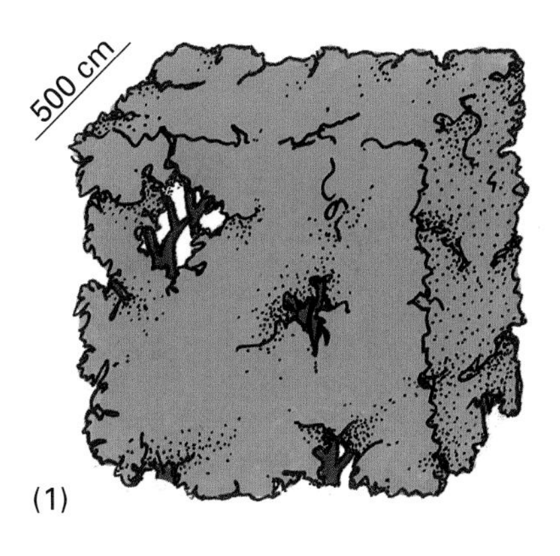

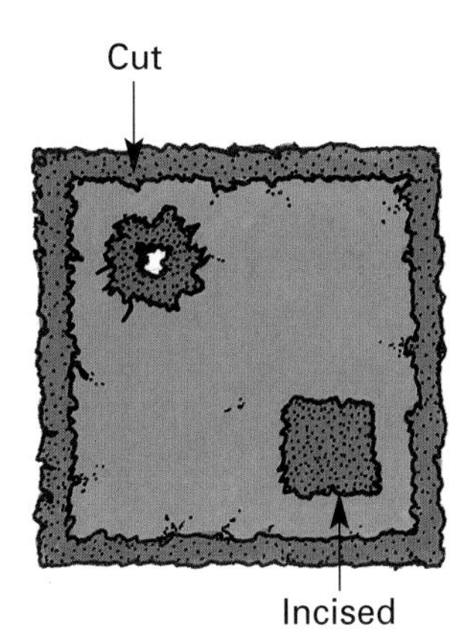

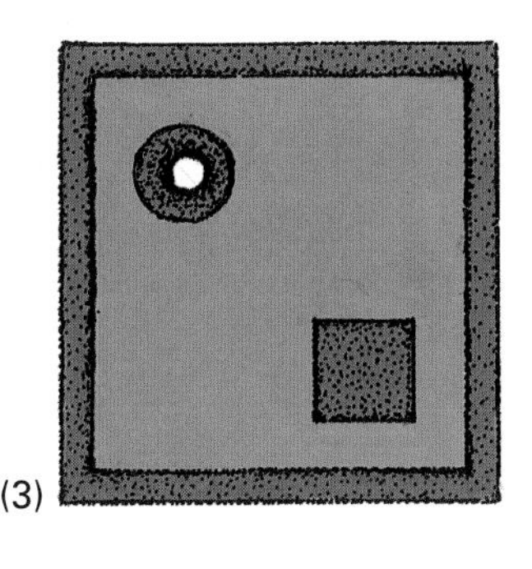

Surface decoration in yew: 'Nicholson' wall with peep hole

Based on Ben Nicholson's abstract garden sculpture, this yew piece is in fact a tightly clipped rectangle incised and pierced with a peephole. Halfway down a lawn and to one side it adds a distinctive note to a garden. The peep-hole is a homage to a world that is constantly viewed through a camera lens.

1. Grow the rectangular yew buttress to approximately 2m×50cm (6.5×1.5ft), which takes some time, but three or four large plants could achieve this in three years. Encourage the peep-hole from the start by keeping the approximate area free of growth.

2. Detail is added when you clip the yew. Create the recessed frame by clipping the edge further back by 3cm (1in). Keep the peep-hole clear and balance it by cutting a rectangle into the new growth further back than the surface of the central square.

3. This is an idea for brightening up the surface of a hedge as well as for creating a single buttress. Art in the garden is the application of experience felt elsewhere to the world of plant growth and living green form that is encouraged around our homes.

arch with a bridge lower down. The letter B would require a backpiece as the vertical and the two curves trained around the supporting frame, and so on. Numbers can be created in a similar way.

As with any framework it would need to last until the woody material of the letter has hardened up and the support can be dispensed with. Again use a soft string as a tying material to prevent damage.

BIRDS

A traditional topiary favourite, often seen as free-standing specimens or as finials on the tops of cuboid bases or cones, topiary birds tend to belong to a unique class of bird. Topiary peacocks are traditional and aspirational and also much welcomed as a fun feature.

The initial B for Bagot (the family surname) growing over its frame, in an old postcard from Levens Hall.

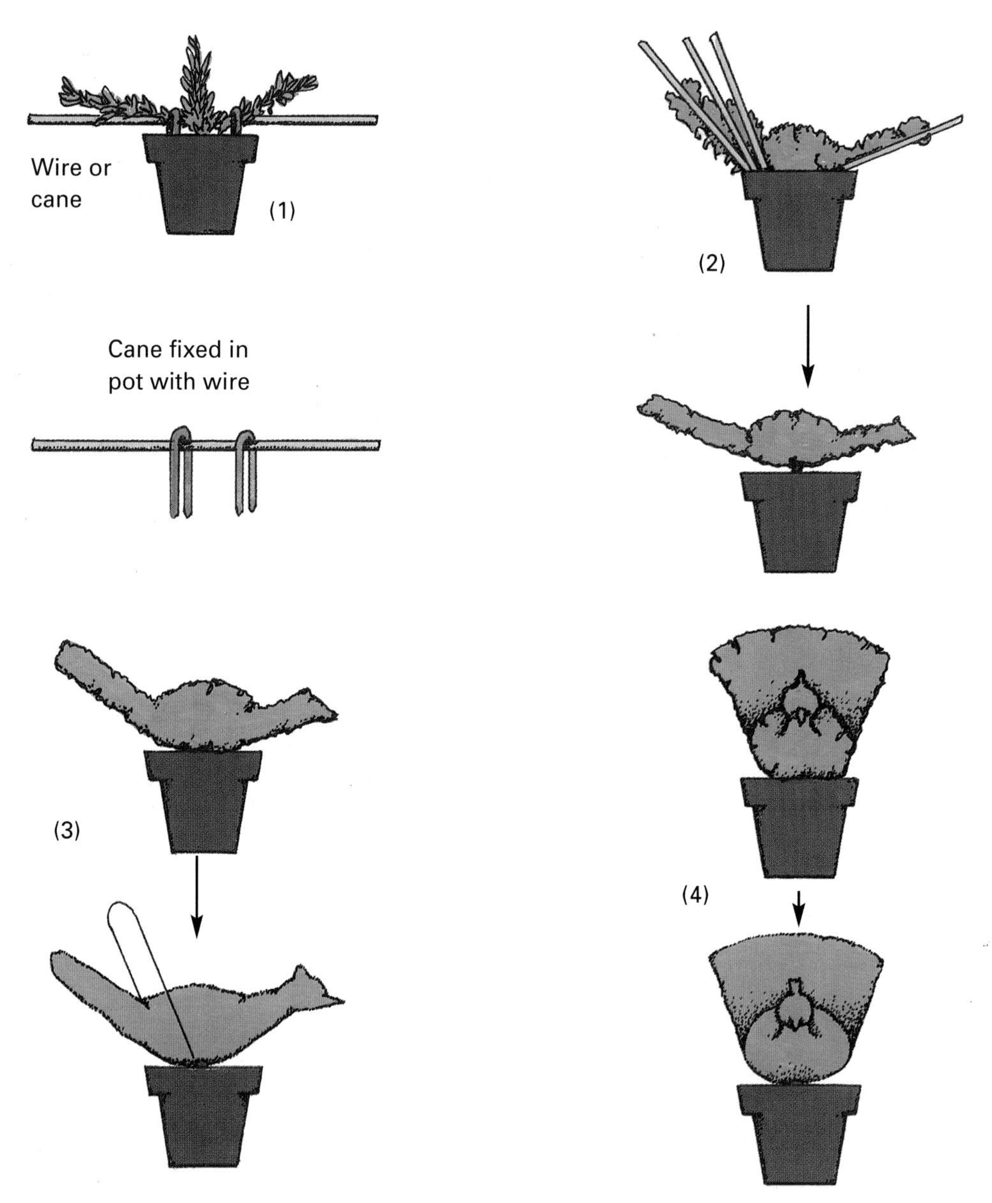

Topiary peacocks in pots

With house moving more frequent these days, most people would want to make sure that their carefully trained and clipped topiary peacock was able to move with them, and that is why a pot is suggested. For yew the pot would have to be quite large, close to 1m (3ft) in diameter.

1. The yew plant to use here is a single hedging piece, and you will need at least three clear shoots. Plant it in the centre of the pot and secure it to a horizontal cane using wire loops. Allow the central yew shoot to grow upwards to form the body of the peacock. One shoot is directed and loosely tied with twine to the horizontal cane to form the head and neck. The third shoot can either be trained horizontally to create a non-displaying bird or attached to a sloping cane to create the start of the fan.

2. You will need to be patient while the yew grows in the desired directions. Encourage the fan to branch out, inserting extra canes if necessary.

3. You can begin shaping roughly after about three or four years.

4. The bird will only ever roughly look like the classic peacock of topiary tradition, but each year as it grows more detail can be clipped into it. The important point is that the creator can be proud of it, as proud as a peacock, in fact!

There are two traditional forms, one with a vertically set fanned out tail which is the displaying peacock; the other with an elongated, horizontal tail rather more reminiscent of a pheasant. To form one of these birds, supporting material is required in the short term to train the plant growth in four different directions. One group at 45 degrees will form the neck and head, the head being bent down as growth permits using a string line. Two groups at either side of the body will form wings if required and the last group of branches is trained to form the tail, whether horizontal or vertical. With more growth over time the details can be improved upon and the proportions adjusted. Clipping will, of course, encourage infilling growth and the bird will take shape. Topiary birds are traditionally made of yew but other plants may be tried.

ANIMALS

Historically topiary seems to have left very few subjects excluded from at least an approximation to living creatures of all kinds. Accounts describe elephants, humans, dogs, horses and snails (a variation on the spiral) and these are a challenge today to the new topiarist seeking perhaps one original conversation piece in the garden. The forms which result are of course impressionistic and caricatures to a great degree, which emphasizes the fun element.

Box squirrel offset by bark chippings.

Strong wire or metal frames will be needed in the early stages and these may helpfully convey the intended appearance of the finished creation to acting as a guide. Whether bought or home-made,

Elephant and Mickey Mouse, detail.

An amorphous duck. Even the barest approximation to a representational form works on the eyes and in cartoon simplicity evokes at least a smile.

The model and his topiary portrait.

they will eventually be disguised by the plant growth and clipping will need to be done with hand tools to avoid entanglement with the framework.

Creatures can be made using different plants in order to emphasize colouristic effects and texture; for example golden or variegated plants will help suggest stripes if a tiger is the animal being created. Lonicera (*Lonicera nitida*) comes in golden and variegated forms with small leaves, and, as it responds well to dense clipping, is perhaps the most plastic of topiary subjects.

When the shape begins to be more plant than framework, the amalgamation of separate plants to form bodies on top of four or two legs should be clipped hard to maintain the desired result. Long growth can be left in places to effect texture.

Most of this work will be freehand and develop over time. With luck and the application of the principles of topiary a rich variety of figures is possible.

CLOUD AND ABSTRACT SCULPTURAL SHAPES

The billowing effect of cloud pruning is becoming popular now in Western gardens. Always a part of

Close-up detail of lonicera responding to wire training.

the Oriental gardening tradition, it adds a lightness of touch to the garden as well as the challenge and pleasure of creating it. Abstraction in sculpture inevitably has led to abstract topiary. Low, flowing hedges undulating along the side of a path in a garden add a sense of rhythm in greenery that is calming and welcoming. Modern formal gardens are an invitation to install or create abstract plant sculpture, which may have stunning results.

Abstraction can derive from existing, untrimmed plants being gently shaped into curving forms. This gives results very speedily, delivering a finished product at the pace of contemporary life. At the same time, the results are mellowing and meditative, cool and calming, and their effect is not reliant upon perfection of form or symmetry but upon a boldness of touch which cannot be faulted. More traditional topiary shapes all too easily display their faults.

The same rules apply to these forms as to the more traditional shapes: ensure that all trimmed surfaces are exposed to maximum light by making your sculptures wider at the base.

In topiary almost anything is possible. Its application is self-expanding and infectious, bounded only by the limits of your imagination. The topiarist learns as he clips and creates as he clips, whether by following a formal symmetrical shape or by softening natural plant growth to a merging flux of abstract forms.

A three-century-old tiered piece just about maintains its vertical dignity in the topiary garden at Levens. This piece is reminiscent of oriental cloud topiary where it is viewed against the sky.

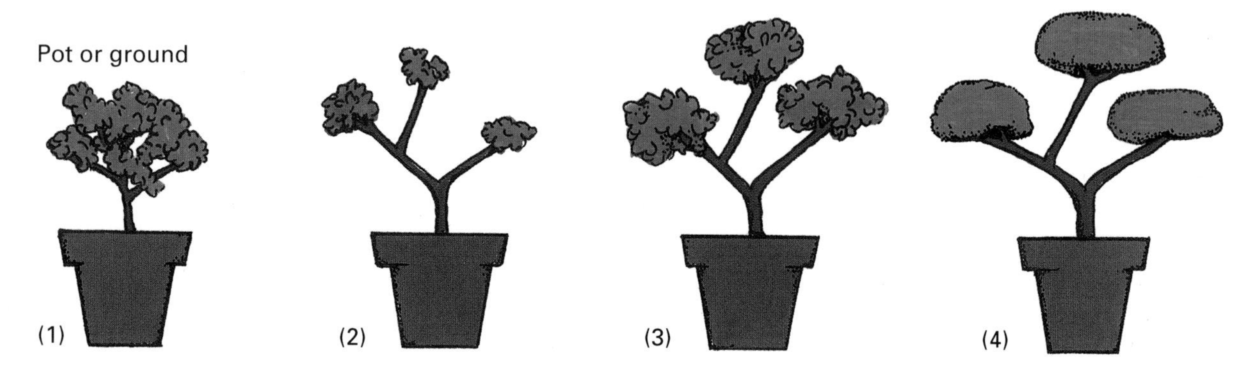

Cloud topiary in box

Cloud topiary is essentially a variation on, and an abstraction from, standard topiary.

1. Choose a box plant or cutting with three or four clear stems, preferably with one breaking out of another half way up.

2. Following the principles for standard formation, keep the stems clean of side shoots and allow the tips to grow until a pleasing configuration is arrived at.

3. When the desired height (for the site or the container) is achieved the stems are cleaned and the tips pinched out to encourage bushy cloud shapes.

4. Clip these tightly to create terminal clouds. Keep the shapes flattened unless a bunch of balloons is the required effect.

Racehorse and jockey in a pot.

CHAPTER 10

Special Projects

REJUVENATION

There comes a time in the life of all topiary when drastic measures are required to give them a new lease of life. All gardeners face this problem with trees and shrubs in their care and the topiarist is no exception. It may be that a piece has simply outgrown the space allotted to it – overgrowing a pathway, blocking the light or view from a window. It may be that its dense, heavy surface is now so far away from the supporting trunk that the shape gives way to sagging. (In natural growth, foliage weight is distributed along horizontal branches by decreasing towards the outer tips.) It may be that the shape itself has become old, thin and threadbare and beyond basic maintenance through annual clipping. Whatever the problem, bold and decisive remedial action is required.

The most popular topiary plant, yew, fortunately responds extremely well to very hard cutting back

Cleaning out the heart of an ancient specimen.

Restoring an outgrown piece to order.

New growth on an old trunk showing the rejuvenative powers of yew.

even on very old specimens. Reduced back to bare, thick, old trunks it will almost immediately begin to sprout new growth, so reduction in its dimensions to promote rejuvenation can be recommended with total confidence. This operation should take place in spring when the new growing season begins. The principle is to cut back the growth until the thickest branches and trunk at the centre of the plant are exposed. Rather than undertake this work all at one go it is better to carry it out over a couple of seasons as this operation inflicts a huge, traumatic shock on the living plant. If you are rejuvenating a hedge, only deal with one side during a single season. With specimen topiary, treat one side and most importantly the top and uppermost parts one year, leaving the remaining side until after successful regenerative growth is visible and thriving.

With some shapes and settings, however, the whole piece will have to be reduced at once. This is usually quite successful too, if not ideal, but it has to be borne in mind that whichever method is chosen some plants may not survive.

After reduction treatment it is essential to feed the plants well and to water if necessary. This helps to ease the stress and encourage new growth which appears all over the bare trunks as if sprayed on and is always surprising to behold. Yews are often regarded as symbols of longevity, and it is this enduring life force which shows itself during rejuvenation. Then the training can start again with either a reduced version of the original design or a different one. What actually happens is that the topiarized specimen is returned to being a single-stemmed plant; it loses all the design imposed upon it and becomes a fresh candidate for the topiarist.

Box, which is the second most frequently used plant in topiary, will also respond well to severe pruning.

This is how drastically yew can be cut back in order to generate new growth and restore its topiary form.

Cutting into old yew.

New growth breaking from the base of a bare trunk.

Flanking yew 'gateposts' cut back and beginning to sprout new growth.

A renewed pyramid sprouts in a historic setting. This drastic treatment was meted out to a 300-year-old specimen.

Often after years of slowly growing and developing, topiary's more detailed featuring becomes a little lost or blurred. Parts can grow one into another and sharp angles become more rounded. If drastic rejuvenation does not appear to be the answer then the topiary specimen can be sharpened up significantly by careful, detailed work with secateurs: defining lines more clearly, separating merged surface planes and removing shoots which by overlapping or growing out of the constraints of the design have contributed to its loss of clear definition. This detailed work in fine-tuning the topiary will improve its appearance immeasurably and is an immensely satisfying job for the topiary artist.

Where specimens have become very large and over-mature and are beginning to look thin and weedy, drastic reduction will often return them to their earlier strength of form and vigour. Overgrowth is a strain on the root system, which is why top growth becomes weak and spindly, and severe cutting back redresses the balance.

PROPAGATION

This essential and important aspect of horticulture does not really appertain to the art of topiary as the enthusiast is more likely to want to begin with as large a plant as possible for the creation of specimen topiary. With the renewal of interest in topiary the enthusiast is currently well catered for by garden centres and specialist nurseries. The size of plants bought will always be reflected in their price, of course. Paying more, however, for a larger or taller plant does mean that extra years of growth are there to play with from the outset.

Growing trees and shrubs from seeds is the most natural form of propagation and is more likely to be used by the bonsai enthusiast wishing to begin training and conditioning plants from their germination as seedlings.

Taking cuttings is a vegetative and relatively simple way to clone plants, and it may well be that if ivy is used as a soft topiary material for covering frames and netting shapes then it is propagated to increase the number of specimens created using a particular variety of ivy. Ivy roots easily and grows quickly.

In one area of topiary gardening propagation by cuttings is quite often practised. Box in large quantities can pro rata work out to be a considerable expense. As it roots easily, if rather slowly, gardeners may wish to increase the amount of box edging in their gardens or specimen topiary in pots by taking cuttings; the results grow quite fast. There are also a large number of different box cultivars and species and favoured ones may be rooted and exchanged within the gardening and topiary community.

As with all vegetative propagation, it is a race between rooting below the ground and rotting or dying off above the ground. The aim is therefore to create the optimum conditions for rooting and win the race. When taking cuttings from box it is well to remember that vertically growing shoots are preferable to those inclining towards the horizontal plane, as these may continue to do so when rooted. Vertical shoots are leaders and having grown atop the plant in the light are well resourced with nutrients and contain the food reserves within their tissues to create strong and healthy rooted cuttings.

CONTAINER GROWING

From the symmetrically paired bay laurel trees flanking a Georgian doorway to a table-top spiral of ivy grown on wire, container-grown topiary is a decorative and effective way of using trained and clipped plants. In more formal or harder landscapes or in the absence of any garden space at all – and indeed in temporary conditions such as wedding marquees and table decorations – container-grown topiary is a striking and effective way of using the art.

Containers are usually not the kindest conditions under which plants are grown as they can accentuate adverse conditions. Heat, cold, drought, lack of light and damage to the container will all affect the specimens. The garden design needs to provide relatively sheltered locations for container topiary, but with the temporary usage under cover or indoors in mind, one great advantage of container topiary is that, provided it is not too large, it can be moved to better conditions, 'rested' and nursed back up to strength if it has suffered in any way.

While many container plants are annual or considered as easily replaceable, topiary is expensive and in the care of an enthusiast is the result of years of care and training. Awareness of the dangers of adverse conditions is necessary in order to protect and preserve the specimens.

Hard landscaping reflects sunlight and heat and lowers humidity around the containers while the proximity of walls and buildings can funnel drying air currents. In very cold weather the roots of the plant are not snugly underground but may indeed end up frozen solid in the container. Positions chosen should be sheltered as much as possible from extremes of heat, wind and frost.

Container-grown plants require that the topiarist provides all of their needs in terms of watering and feeding. In every sense they are as vulnerable as indoor plants even if by their nature hardy. There is no escape from the container for roots to seek water and eventually the specimen will become pot-bound and will need to be potted on to a larger container – or planted out into the garden, where the same principles of planting out apply as for any newly bought container-grown specimen.

Finally, one of the great delights of container-grown topiary plants is their manoeuvrability. They can be carried around the garden to an ideal location as seen from a particular point of view. They can be arranged in groups and shuffled around to prevent over-familiarity. They can be given as presents. They can also be rotated regularly to even up growth on all sides.

GARDENING WITH TOPIARY

There are as many ways of gardening with topiary as there are gardeners. Topiary may be a single feature, subservient to the garden design as a whole, or it may become dominant in the garden of a dedicated topiary enthusiast. As in the garden of Pliny the Younger two thousand years ago, part or all of the garden could become a topiary landscape filled with clipped specimens of different species, sizes and shapes whether formal, abstract or figurative. From classical, traditional topiary as found in historic houses to new topiary, there is a whole range of approaches and created effects. Topiary can immediately create the feel of a traditional, English cottage garden. It can echo a grander style. With new topiary it can be an exploration of new approaches to garden design and be forward-looking or at least contemporary.

Rising out of gravel or paving and out of that endangered species, the front lawn, it can in one bold stroke create a sense of place, ownership, care and style that immediately distinguishes and upgrades a property.

Levens Hall has a traditional topiary garden in a unique historic setting. At the same time, however, it offers inspiration to new topiary by the juxtaposition and contrasting of different shapes and heights. Above eye-level it is a textured profile against the skyline that Pliny the Younger might recognize, but that a contemporary designer might seek to emulate in a more abstract fashion.

At ground level blocks of planting are an integral part of the topiary garden. Seasonal bedding changed twice a year gives blocks of colour and texture out of which specimen topiary can rise. In spring tulips and pansies provide both colour and a reminder of the topiary garden as historically a Dutch garden. In summer, verbenas, argyranthemums, heliotropes and stocks, to name only a tiny selection, can be laid out in a contemporary massing of coloured plant material to create a total effect. When densely planted these box-edged panels of colour do not detract from the topiary images because the plants perform *en masse* in an almost abstract coloured composition of contrasts. This coloured dimension is a worthy setting for the stars of the show – the topiary pieces themselves. They rise with the dignity and self-assurance of three centuries of continuous performance.

The use of annual bedding plants as a setting guarantees a uniform and continuous flowering. Mixed herbaceous planting would add a note of confusion and fail to perform as well. In smaller gardens, however, the fixed dramatic poses of topiary are more likely to work well rising out of a mixed planting.

These planting accompaniments enhance the topiary and, as long as they do not impede access for clipping or compete with young topiary for water and nutrients, make for a harmonious association on any scale.

CHAPTER 11

Problem-Solving

Because topiary is generally created from hardy plant material, often native, as in the case of yew, few serious problems tend to occur – as long as the principles of preparation, positioning and planting are respected and adhered to. That said, all plants have pests, predators and diseases although they also have in-built resistance and defence mechanisms. The goal of having physically thriving specimens well suited to their environment, which can therefore look after themselves with respect to pests and diseases, is the soundest principle of ecological and environmentally friendly gardening.

PESTS

Each plant species will have its own range of parasites that it is susceptible to, including sap-sucking insects, aphids, scale, leaf miner and gall-forming midges.

On a limited scale, hand picking or clipping off affected parts is the easiest approach; chemical applications are only sensible for large-scale infestations. Topiary species tend to be self-regulating and it might require an expert eye even to detect a problem of which the gardener is unaware, and indeed may not even have to be concerned about.

The best pest control is a healthy plant. Cultural stress, as in lack of water, drying winds or too much feeding, needs to be avoided. Overfeeding in particular is killing with kindness, as excess new, soft growth is an invitation to pests.

DISEASES

Diseases, too, can be plant-specific. To generalize, plants growing under stress are more likely to succumb to disease, whereas those growing vigorously and producing strong growth will be naturally disease-resistant.

Diseases affecting topiary can be divided into two classes – those that affect the foliage and those that affect the roots. One disadvantage of topiary cultivation is that the much-desired dense, close-grown surfaces create close, humid atmospheres within which disease may thrive if the plant is affected. There is also an almost solid surface over which the disease can spread.

Perhaps the most devastating disease affecting box is the collection of box blights. These provoke the yellowing, browning or blackening of the foliage, which, apart from being unsightly, can cause new shoots to die back and the plant to eventually die. *Volutella*, the causal agent for the traditional form of box blight, was and still is very serious. Plants can recover. A recently recognized disease, cylindrocladium, can and does kill box topiary and hedging/edging. This is being spread by cultivated plants being brought into the garden. This is a space to watch.

As far as diseases affecting the root systems are concerned, phytopthora is the most significant. Yew, in particular, is highly susceptible to this pathogen. Although bronzing, yellowing and eventual death of the foliage are the unfortunate symptoms, the actual cause lies below ground level, where the root system is being slowly killed. This disease (like many others) is encouraged by wet and waterlogged conditions at the roots, which can be avoided if the site is prepared properly. New plantings are more susceptible, where earth movement in preparation for the planting can alter the drainage structure of the soil. If the drainage problem is remedied then the plants may survive to outgrow the problem as they in turn condition the soil with their root growth and water consumption.

CULTURAL DISORDERS

While good gardening practice in topiary gardening is rewarded by healthy, hardy plants, there are potential problems, not all of which can be blamed on a specific pest or disease. Every gardener has bought a plant, nurtured it and then witnessed sudden death syndrome as the carefully tended beauty gives up the ghost and dies for no apparent reason.

Noticeable poor growth on a topiary specimen may be the fault of many things: too much or too little light; extremes of temperature or rapid temperature fluctuations; shade; water dripping from trees or faulty house guttering; localized severe wind turbulence; localized air humidity (heating outlets from houses may cause this); or dank, dismal conditions. All of these tend to be discovered as causes when it is too late to do very much about them.

If soil nutrient levels in some vital element are low or the pH is wrong, this can be quantified and remedied after soil testing.

Bad drainage as a problem cannot be overemphasized. While the planting area may be prepared to perfection, the surrounding areas may cause water to seep back into it, cancelling out any benefits from careful adherence to planting rules. Compaction of the soil can affect drainage too, whether from people's feet or vehicles. When building work is being undertaken this needs to be watched out for. Competition from other plants also needs to be taken into account.

Topiary gardening on the whole involves gardening with healthy, hardy material. The words above act as a cautionary note. Good initial soil preparation and careful location of plants invariably guarantee success. To be interested in topiary and take up the challenge and practise it is to become involved with an aspect of gardening that has survived, thrived and flourished despite the vagaries of taste and the trials of time for over two thousand years.

Useful Addresses

TOPIARY SOCIETIES

The European Boxwood and Topiary Society
c/o EBTS Membership Secretary
Toft Monks
The Hithe
Rodborough Common
Stroud
Gloucestershire GL5 5BN

The American Boxwood Society
www.boxwoodsociety.org

TOPIARY PLANTS

United Kingdom

Earlstone Box and Topiary
Earlstone Manor Farm
Burghclere, Newbury
Berkshire RG20 9NG
Tel 01635 278648
www.earlstoneboxandtopiary.co.uk

Highfield Hollies
Highfield Farm, Hatch Lane
Liss
Hampshire GU33 7NH
Tel 01730 892372
e-mail:louise@highfieldhollies.com
www.highfieldhollies.com

Pound Hill Plants
West Kington Nurseries
Chippenham
Wiltshire SN14 7JG
Tel 01249 783880
www.poundhillplants.co.uk

River Garden Nurseries
Troutbeck
Otford
Sevenoaks
Kent TN14 5PH
Tel 01959 525588
e-mail: box@river-garden.co.uk
www.river-garden.co.uk

The Romantic Garden Nursery
Swannington
Norwich NR9 5NW
Tel 01603 261488
e-mail: enquiries@romantic-garden.nursery.co.uk
www.romantic-garden.nursery.co.uk

USA

Chris's Topiary Nursery
Riverside
California
Tel (909) 352 3526
e-mail: mrtopiary@charter.net

The Topiary Store
16307 115th Avenue SW
Vashon Island
WA 98070
Tel (206) 567 5047
e-mail: topiarysales@cs.com

TOOLS AND ACCESSORIES

United Kingdom

Henchman Platforms
Haygate Engineering Co. Ltd
Manor Farm
Hannington
Tadley
Hampshire RG26 5TG
Tel 01635 299847
e-mail:consumerhelp@henchman.co.uk
www.henchman.co.uk

Topiary Frames by Brian Joyce
9 Ash Grove
Wheathampstead
Herts AL4 8DF
Tel 01582 629724

USA

Greenpiece Wire Art
PO Box 260
Bridge Station
Niagara Falls
NY 14305
Tel (905) 679 6066
e-mail: info@greenpiecewireart.com
www.greenpiecewireart.com

Kenneth Lynch and Sons, Inc.
84 Danbury Road
PO Box 488
Wilton
Connecticut
Tel (203) 762 8363
e-mail: info@klynchandsons.com
www.klynchandsons.com

Noah's Ark Topiary
PO Box 10213
Largo
Fl 33773
www.noahsark.topiary.com

TOPIARY COURSES

Judy Older
Wykhurst Topiary
Wykhurst
Mill Road
Aldington
Kent TN25 7AJ
Tel 01233 720395
e-mail: judyoldertopiary@yahoo.co.uk

Index